Release the Poet Within!

How to Launch and Improve Poetry Craft and Ministry

Leona Choy

Release the Poet Within!

How to Launch and Improve Poetry Craft and Ministry

Leona Choy

Golden Morning Publishing
Winchester, Virginia

Release the Poet Within!: *How to Launch and Improve Poetry Craft and Ministry*
© 1996 Leona Choy
Produced by Richard Choy

Published by *Golden Morning Publishing*
P.O. Box 2697, Winchester, VA 22604

Library of Congress Cataloging-in-Publication Data

Choy, Leona
      Release the Poet Within! How to Launch and Improve
      Poetry Craft and Ministry

ISBN 1-889283-02-9
      1. Non-fiction—Writing craft—Christianity

Published in the United States of America

Printed in the USA by

MORRIS
PUBLISHING
3212 E. Hwy 30
Kearney, NE 68847
800-650-7888

Books by Leona Choy

Authored, edited or collaborated,
including foreign language editions

A Call To The Church From Wang Mingdao
Andrew Murray, Apostle Of Abiding Love.
      Spanish, Dutch, Chinese, Afrikaans, Korean editions
Christiana Tsai. Also Chinese edition
Divine Applications (poetry)
Heart Cry Of China. Also Chinese edition
His Mighty Power/Esther Wang
Heaven and Nature Sing (poetry)
The Holy Spirit and His Work/A.B.Simpson
Hospital Gowns Don't Have Pockets:
      Why me? What now?
How to Capture and Develop Ideas for Writing
Improving Our Cross-cultural Postures:Missions on the Level
The Inner Chamber/Andrew Murray (Contemporized)
Jewels From The Queen Of The Dark Chamber/
      Christiana Tsai. Also in Chinese.
The Key To The Missionary Problem/Andrew Murray
      (Contemporized). Nigerian and Portuguese editions
Life—Stop Crowding Me! (poetry)
Let My People Go!/Moses C.Chow with Leona Choy
No Ground/Evelyn Carter Spencer with Leona Choy
On Your Mark: A Christian Traveler's Guide to China
Powerlines. Also Chinese and Korean editions
Release the Poet Within!
      How to Launch and Improve Poetry Craft and Ministry
Singled Out for God's Assignment: A Widow's Valley of Learning
Songs of My Pilgrimage (poetry)
The State Of The Church/Andrew Murray (Contemporized)
Touching China: Close Encounters of the Christian Kind
The Widow's Might: Strength from the ROCK
My Dreams and Visions:Autobiography. Ted Choy with Leona Choy
Celebrate This Moment! (poetry) Trilogy

About the Author

Born of Czech parents in Iowa and a graduate of Wheaton College, Illinois, Leona Choy served with her late husband, Ted, in mission, church and educational work in Hong Kong, Singapore, China and the United States. Co-founder of *Ambassadors For Christ, Inc.*, a campus ministry for Chinese university students and scholars, her quarter century of work was administrative and editorial.

Fourteen trips to the People's Republic of China as guide/escort and English teaching consultant enriched her research and experiences for writing. As President of WTRM-FM *(Southern Light Gospel Music Network)* in the Shenandoah Valley of Virginia, Leona produced a daily radio program for five years.

Author, editor or collaborator of over 25 published books and 12 foreign language editions, her articles have appeared in over 70 different periodicals. Leona's poems have been published in scores of magazines and read over her daily radio programs, *Intensive Care,* and *Living It Up* on WTRM.

She is managing editor of *Golden Morning Publishing* in Winchester, Virginia, where she makes her home. Four grown sons and seven grandchildren keep her busy when she isn't writing or traveling.

Preface

"Something has happened. Poetry is back in the spotlight," according to Michael Bugeja, Poetry Columnist for *Writer's Digest*. In his June 1996 column this professor and author of six volumes of poetry reported some startling developments in American society at large. Because he is one of the foremost spokespersons for the art and craft of poetry today and author of a book on that subject, I quote his insightful observations of the poetry scene:

> As writers were predicting poetry's demise in such cultural magazines as *Harper's*, rap artists began restoring the oral tradition. Soon after, rap reawakened the ancient art of performance poetry. Then serious writers began composing verse for the ear. Cowboy poetry began attracting thousands at annual readings in the Southwest. Slams became the rage in New York and Chicago. By the early 1990s, poetry was going public at state fairs and presidential inaugurations.
>
> Today poetry is being created and exchanged at home via PC and modem. Major online services feature poetry forums, "cafes" and "salons." You can even enjoy poetry via multimedia CD-ROM.
>
> Why this interest in something so many in the '70s said was terminally ill . . . and television was killing it? Why this passion for something so many in the '80s said had been forgotten, said was never popular to begin with, said academe had conducted the autopsy?
>
> Young scholars say poetry is making a comeback precisely because money has *nothing* to do with it. You can't earn a living as a poet. But you can profit

as a person by composing poems. It's that noncommercial aspect that more and more people are finding so appealing.

Performance poetry is coming into its own again, agreed prizewinning poet and English professor David Kirby. As there are "stand-up comics" and entertainers today, we see "stand-up poets" again in the oral tradition of the ancient Greeks. Caribbean and African poets still chant their poems aloud today.

Bill Moyers, *Public Broadcasting System* television commentator and author of *The Language of Life,* a celebration of American poetry released as both a book and an eight-part series on PBS, echoed those observations:

"[Poetry is enjoying] its biggest literary renaissance in the United States since the Beat movement of the 1950s and '60s. An enormous range of voices is now getting heard, and they run the full gamut."

He pointed out that coffee-houses, theaters and university lecture programs offer poetry readings to thousands of appreciative listeners. In New York City alone some poets present their work in 150 different venues. In Moyers' television documentary the poets accompany their readings with jazz, the blues and various forms of folk music. Agreeing that ours is a culture where it's all but impossible to be a professional poet, Moyers stated:

> This is the anomaly. There is very little income attached to poetry, so poets are free to speak what is in their hearts. They write the truth because they are liberated by penury. They are not like politicians who are going to be rewarded by the applause of the

crowd; they are not like advertisers who try to sell you something. [Poetry is] the most honest language I hear today.

Is poetry written by Christians beginning to flourish in our American society? Are poetry readings and workshops in the Christian context becoming popular?

If not, why not?

Are Christians among the serious poetry writers composing quality crafted "verses for the ear" whose work is respected by the academic community?

If not, why not?

How about "verses for the King" in the model of Psalm 45:1? "My heart overflows with a good theme; I address my verses to the King; my tongue is the pen of a ready writer."

Do poets who are Christians reach out with eager "hearts overflowing" to the man on the street with down-to-earth yet uplifting "good themes"?

If not, why not?

Poetry isn't an art form that is intrinsically tainted or defiled by the world. It is a pure, innocent artistic expression that some godly men and women have written through the ages. Why have so many contemporary Christians largely abandoned it?

Prose writing is a neutral medium which can be used for good or evil, for pride or the glory of God and the encouragement of man. Christians don't abandon prose simply because it may be misused. Poetry is a similar literary medium. We can use the word in print in any format for positive purposes or for ill. We can claim it for God as we write to advance His Kingdom. We can exalt the Eternal Word who was made flesh through the written word *in both prose and poetry.*

This book is a modest but sincere effort to address this situation. I want to motivate Christians who are endowed by God with a poetic gift of expression to improve and enrich the quality of their poetry, to hone their verse to be artistically acceptable—"in favor with man."

More than that, I challenge poets who are Christians to use their gift for ministry—to be "in favor with God."

We honor God, as Jesus did, if we "grow in wisdom and stature and *in favor with God and man.*"

Foreword

Almost everyone has tried to write a poem at one time or another. The poem seems to burst out either as an expression of great joy or unbearable grief. As a result, some have notebooks full of their efforts. Others pack them away in an old trunk or storage box.

We can't bear to throw out our poems, but we don't think they are worthwhile to show to anyone else. Dashing off a poem may be easy, but *writing what would be considered a good poem is difficult.*

Leona Choy has come to our rescue.

She reminds us that even great poets don't receive their treasured poetic thoughts complete, perfect and saleable. We need to work and rework the basic nuggets until they shine with mysterious beauty.

Leona believes in excellence, and she is not content to keep its secrets to herself. She is committed to sharing them with others and is willing to answer the hard questions for us:

Are poets born or made?
What is the difference between a good poem and one that need improvement?
How can I improve my writing?
Does anyone actually *buy* poetry these days?
How can I share my poems with others?
Can my poetry become a ministry to others?

Leona is well qualified to answer these and many more questions for us. For poets who are serious about their craft, or want to be, her book is a must.

Roberta Kells Dorr
Novelist and sometime poet

Introduction

Do you have a "Muse" somewhere within you? Many of us have some degree of poetic tendency or aptitude which we either try to express or suppress.

Defined by the dictionary, a Muse is "the genius or powers characteristic of a poet." Written in lower case, a *muse* is "the power regarded as inspiring a poet." The word originated in Greek mythology and referred to any of the nine daughters of Zeus and Mnemosyne who presided over the various arts. Calliope, for example, was the goddess daughter in charge of epic poetry, and Erato was the muse who inspired lyric poetry. A*mus*ement and *mus*eum come from the same root meaning.

In this book I *don't* use the term in a metaphysical way but simply to describe our propensity, leaning, talent or gift of expressing ourselves in poetry. I call that inclination "the poet within." No New Age connotation intended. For the poet who is a Christian, "the power regarded as inspiring a poet" is God. He also gave the gift to use it as ministry.

I remember a common saying from my childhood. After someone by chance rhymed two words, we would tease and chant, "You're a poet and don't know it, but your feet show it—they're Longfellows!" Humor aside, some of us who write poetry might confess, "I'm a poet, but reluctant to show it!"

Why do some of us hide the fact that we write poetry and never *release the poet within?*

"Poetry—merely whispering its name frightens

everyone away. It can send grown men scurrying to the other end of the reception hall or plunge a pleasant airplane conversation into thunderous silence," observed Rita Dove, Poet Laureate of the United States. This Pulitzer Prize winner was reluctant for years to admit that her main interest and career choice centered on poetry.

Why?

"There are a thousand and one myths about artists in general and poets in particular that make it difficult to be taken seriously," Rita wrote in a *Writer's Digest* article. During her graduate work and later teaching in a university, Rita hedged the inevitable question, "What do you do for a living?" Finally, she decided to let the chips fall where they may and declared, "I'm a poet. I write poetry. If people regard me as peculiar ... so be it."

I understand her reticence. From childhood I wrote poetry because of an inner compulsion. *Mother Goose* rhymes initiated me into the world of verse, and I tried to imitate them by making up my own rhymes. One Christmas when I was seven, an aunt gave me the thick, illustrated volume of Stevenson's *A Child's Garden of Verses*. It sparked into flame my desire to write poetry. I memorized many poems effortlessly because of their singsong format and my repeated reading. I recited poems while pumping up on my rope swing under our old apple tree in the back yard.

Without brothers and sisters for playmates, I chose books as my close friends. After I saved enough nickels and dimes to buy the paperback edition of *One Hundred and One Famous Poems,* Wordsworth, Longfellow, Byron and Dickinson became my friends. My favorite card game as a child was "Authors." Poets' portraits and their works were pictured on the playing cards. Our local newspaper published Edgar Guest's whimsical poetry. I devoured his books on folksy topics which I understood more easily than the more obscure themes of the classic poets. I can recite his poem, *Myself*, to this day:

> I have to live with myself and so
> I want to be fit for myself to know;
> I want to be able, as days go by
> always to look myself straight in the eye....

Our family was not particularly literary, although my beloved live-in Czech grandmother who didn't speak a word of English loved poetry in her own language. When I snuggled on her lap on long evenings, she read to me in the Czech language. She taught me to recite a few traditional Czech poems which I still remember.

I tried to write my own poems. Because I was so shy, I never let anyone know or see them. None of my classmates wrote them, and I was afraid of being ridiculed. I thought the other children would call me the equivalent of a "nerd" in today's slang. I longed to meet a *live* poet who wrote about ideas in my world.

I hid my "collected works" in a musty suitcase in the attic. When I reached my teens, I decided to burn all my poems in a ritual of relinquishment because, to my newly grown up mind, they were too juvenile. But I couldn't keep from writing poetry because it bubbled up from somewhere inside.

I have always found it more natural to express my emotions in poetry than prose. I was delighted when we started to study poetry in a high school literature class. But when my interpretation of some classic poem differed from the teacher's explanation, she told me it was "wrong" and I felt humiliated. I wondered how she could really know what the poet meant. Her remark kept me hiding my poetic efforts so that no one would criticize them.

Why are some of us as adults still self-conscious about writing poems? Are we afraid to expose our inner thoughts and show our vulnerability? Why does a poetry workshop at a writers' conference seem to have a different ambience? Is it because writing poetry is uniquely individual, more subjective and illusive than writing nonfiction, novels or short stories? Some of us sign up almost secretly for a poetry workshop.

Perhaps we are embarrassed because some people view poets unfairly as ivory tower dwellers, eccentric and not in touch with the real world. They think we still write with quill pens and live in garrets.

It's time to write about our contemporary world in modern language and address today's concerns. We should be proud of our honorable craft. I advocate that today's poets stand up and declare without apology, *"My name is [   ] and I'm a poet!"* If you have *ever* written a poem, be bold and write your name in the brackets!

If we are poets and Christians, poetry may be one of our ministry gifts. Let us consider that possibility. Whether beginners or seasoned poets, we should continue to improve our skills and discipline ourselves to write *better* poetry for the glory of God. Our poetry ministry is a high calling for which we need God's enabling.

I intend this book to be *user friendly* and open new vistas of understanding and inspiration for you. Whether as an information-refresher for your techniques or a challenge for ministry through poetry, may it serve as a launching pad for your joyful journey into expanded poetic expression.

Let's encourage one another to *release the creative muse within us!*

———————

Author's note:

Throughout this book I used my own poems for most of the poetry examples. That was simply a convenient way to illustrate certain aspects of our craft.

Contents

Poem: Barren Pen

Off the Launching Pad!

Bibliography and Resources
An Invitation for Critique/Ordering Information

Barren Pen

I write
to express my soul
etch joys in ink
distill tears in print
give shape to dreams
deliver pregnant thoughts.

When I am *full*
I sing
I write
my heart overflows
I cannot restrain
my prolific pen.

When I am *empty*
my soul lies limp
my heart is sterile
blank paper stares at me
my thoughts lie covered
by a blanket of snow.
I languish
passive and stagnant
scarce noting the passing
of futile, flat days.
Impotent and unproductive
my spirit wanders
in a desert wasteland.

Lord, save me
from a barren pen!
Deliver my mind
from its empty womb.
Let me bear Your thoughts
into life as I birth them
through my ready pen.

Leona Choy

*S*urprisingly, poetry preceded prose in history, and it was the first to be put in writing. Early man depended on oral tradition. Because poetry had rhythm, people memorized it more easily than narrative prose. Minstrels recited folk tales in poetry with a musical accompaniment. Folk wisdom, tales of tribal heroes, religious teachings, philosophies and history were transmitted in poetic form.

1

The Case for Poetry

It's time we rediscover poetry as "the most beautiful, impressive, and widely effective mode of saying things," as Matthew Arnold described it. Edgar Allan Poe said that poetry was "the rhythmical creation of beauty in words."

*P*oetry deserves a better reputation. People who are apprehensive of poetry may not have read any poetry since teachers forced them to memorize *"Invictus"* in eighth grade.

Some people avoid poetry because they don't understand it. Others think it's not about real life, it's old-fashioned, the language is weird and one needs to be a Ph.D. to decipher the stuff. Granted, some poetry in literature textbooks with its archaic language and obscure themes may be hard to understand, therefore modern readers don't appreciate it. But that shouldn't be grounds to paint all poetry with a negative brush.

Samuel Johnson called poetry the art of uniting pleasure with truth. Alexander Pope agreed. "The truth shines the brighter clad in verse."

If we want to read good contemporary poetry as well as the masters of the past, contemporary poets must write it. Ralph Waldo Emerson said that all men are poets at heart. If that is true, many people have not "released their poet within." If we fail to encourage today's potential poets in their craft, this generation will miss a vital component of its culture. Future generations will be poorer for our neglect.

Nelson A. Rockefeller declared, "A civilization is judged, in a large measure, by its poets. It is they who express a nation's highest, deepest and most beautiful ideas. Without our poets, our culture would hardly deserve the name of culture."

Christian poets are in good company

It is time for Christian poetry to come into its own, and poets who are Christians to take their writing out of the desk drawer. We are in godly company: David, the Israeli king, the brave and virile military leader, was a poet *par excellence*. He compiled his poetry and song lyrics into an anthology with other poets like Asaph, the

Sons of Korah, Solomon, Moses and Ethan. According to the Greek Septuagint, the collection we call *The Psalter* possibly also includes the poetry of Haggai and Zechariah. Solomon wrote 3,000 proverbs and 1,005 songs, according to First Kings chapter four.

Hebrew poetry did not rhyme. Hebrew poets repeated thoughts in parallel clauses using personification, drama, metaphors and similes as poetic devices. They wrote of their experiences, the history of the nation, reflections on life as well as practical proverbs and great divine truths. Many Hebrew poems were prayers and praise set to choral music. Some arose from personal joys and adversities, others from national distress.

As poets who are Christians, let us join that distinguished company and express the poetic gift within us.

Reasons for writing poetry

Seldom today does a poet deliberately write a poem to make money. We soon learn that we are not going to eat caviar and retire early on income from our poems! We shouldn't quit our job or leave our supporting spouse to become a full time poet. I suggest skipping money as a motive for writing poetry. Whatever compensation an editor may send us for publishing our poem, we should count as pocket money, postage money or "mad money" at most. Consider it a bonus if you get anything more than a copy of the publication in which your poem is published.

Marketing a poem to a magazine is generally secondary, a fringe benefit after you study the writers' market guide and discover that a poem you have already written is the kind that a certain periodical might be interested in. Why then do people write poems?

(1) *For catharsis.* Writing provides release, perhaps the venting of an emotion. For many, poetry provides the best medium for such expression. If we don't release an emotion in some way, either a positive or negative way, it can cause us anguish.

Perhaps we should leave deeply personal therapeutic poetry in our desk drawer? We may never need to share it elsewhere. When we wrote the poem it accomplished its purpose—our cathartic expression. We do not rule out marketing, but it is not at the top of our reasons for writing.

(2) *On impulse.* We "feel a poem coming on." That urge sets poetry apart from most prose writing. Poets often write on impulse, when inspired. We don't necessarily know in what direction the poem will take us, but the impulse starts the process.

(3) *To make a statement.* Judson Jerome, former poetry columnist of *Writer's Digest* magazine, a distinguished poet and one of the most widely-read commentators on poetry in this country, described the desire to speak one's mind in poetry as declaring, "I, too, have lived, felt and mattered." We want to verbalize something important about our feelings, express an opinion or set forth a philosophy of life. A poem expresses "us."

(4) *As "verses for the King."* For the Christian poet, a primary reason may be to express deep religious feelings, thoughts, praise or prayer to God. Since such writing is directed to God, it reaches Him and serves its basic

purpose. If we think our poems could have a wider ministry of encouragement, we may share them with friends
and family and Christian groups. Beyond that, we can look
through a writers' market guide for publications which
accept our kind of poetry.

(5) *As an exercise in art form.* This is a legitimate
reason for writing poetry. Some poets choose a conventional pattern like a sonnet, haiku, or iambic pentameter
and then try to think of a subject. They know what structure they want to use, perhaps even outline it as they
would a story. They are exercising their skill, engaging in a
poetry workout.

To practice writing poetry in different forms is like
practicing musical scales. You need to know the basic
elements of your medium before you begin composing
music or writing poetry. You may deviate from rules or
conventional forms only *after* you have learned the funda-
mentals. Creative expression combined with technical
skill has its intrinsic pleasure. Enjoy yourself by "practicing
poetry!"

As poets who are Christians, we should do our
best to convey our thoughts and emotions in quality
writing. E.C. Stedman wrote, "Poetry is an art, and chief
of the fine arts; the easiest to dabble in, the hardest in
which to reach true excellence." We should know the
rules of each art form so we can write well. Careless,
superficial writing doesn't honor the Lord.

(6) *To see our byline.* Do we write and market our
poems primarily to see our work in print and our name
as author? Do we want to be known as poets with the
status symbol it seems to carry? Do we crave applause

from an audience to bolster our self-esteem? All writers, especially poets, like to be recognized. An audience or readership is exhilarating. But as Christian poets, let us not seek recognition as our primary goal.

(7) *To inspire others.* Poets who write in the secular field or publish in literary magazines do not generally try to inspire or uplift others. However, writing inspirational poetry is a valid and important motive for the Christian poet.

(8) *As a ministry for the Lord.* Beyond general inspirational writing is the deeper motive of ministry. Many Christian poems fit that category. The poet sincerely wants to help or influence someone in a positive way, specifically in a Christian way.

Paul Bechtel, former chairman of the Department of English at Wheaton College, advised his classes:

> Rather than thinking of yourself as a Christian poet, call yourself *a poet who is a Christian*. This attitude puts the emphasis first on your art. If you have only Christian sentiments to offer, without art, perhaps you should use prose. The idea in a poem is intensely important, but the form shapes it, gives it significance and clarity.

You don't have to mention God or Jesus in order to write "Christian" poetry. Our Christian philosophy should be evident in all our writing. Good writing is measured by the standard of Philippians 4:8: "Whatever is true, whatever is honorable, whatever is right, whatever is pure, whatever is lovely, whatever is of good repute, if there is any excellence and if anything worthy of praise, let your mind dwell on these things." *And let your poems be about those things, too.*

Larry Brook, in an article on Christian poetry in *Interlit* magazine, stated that expressing faith in a poem should not be a chore nor contrived and obvious:

> [Poetry] is not a vehicle for sending messages. Sermons and telegrams are for messages. Rather, it is an opportunity to express joy, grief, perplexity, praise, awe, loneliness, anger—experiences that color faith. But none of this will work unless we try to be honest and original and concentrate on writing well.

To the casual observer, writing poetry expressing a Christian ideology may seem easy, but Brook says it is incredibly difficult. "All my life I've been trying to write poetry which does not use evangelical rhetoric, but its own particular images that are religious. . . ." Elva McAllaster observed:

> Amateur Christian poets tend, too easily, to write mere echoes: to speak at second hand (or fortieth hand, or forty thousandth!) from expressions long familiar to them through hymns, sermons and testimonies. We must write from our *now*, and we must record the now in fresh ways.

A basketful of potential benefits

Even if you don't pursue poetry writing as your main genre, your effort at writing it has potential benefits:

◆ By exercising your creativity and skill, you improve your prose because you learn to use similes, metaphors and other poetic devices.

◆ As you discipline yourself to repeatedly rewrite the few lines which constitute a poem, you train yourself with transferable skills to apply to other forms of writing. When you hone your poem until it expresses your intention exactly, you develop skills to make you a better fiction writer or journalist.

◆ You learn compact writing, cutting through the superfluous to focus on the core of an idea. In so doing, you become a better editor of your own and other people's writing.

◆ As a poet, you sharpen your senses to observe life more closely, meditate on its meaning and express your responses succinctly.

◆ You learn to love words and play with them like clay, shaping them into something fresh and personal.

◆ Writing poetry helps you know yourself more intimately by drawing your thoughts from the deep well of your experience and background. Poetry aids your personal growth and, perhaps, helps you discover a new identity.

◆ You enjoy the warm and comfortable fellowship of kindred minds through sharing your work with other poets and learning from them. Such stimulation challenges you to scale heights in your experience and expression which you may not have attempted.

◆ Writing poetry opens a wider window to the world. Curiosity impels you to research previously unexplored areas of knowledge and life.

◆ Not the least of the benefits is your personal enjoyment of reading the poetry of others: the great classical poets, contemporary poets and other Christian poets. You appreciate the discipline required to write a good poem and successfully market it, and rejoice in the success of someone whose work made it into print!

◆ Writing poetry gives you a way to expand your present ministry. As you joyfully practice your poetic craft, you will gradually discern whether it is a gift from God and how He wants you to exercise your stewardship.▥

A poet is a nightingale who sits in darkness and sings to cheer its own solitude with sweet sounds. Percy Shelley

*P*oets are all who love, who feel great truths, and tell them. P.J. Bailey

2

How to Identify a Poem and a Poet

Poetry is the spontaneous overflow of powerful feelings. It takes its origin from emotion recollected in tranquility. — William Wordsworth

*P*oetry, like beauty itself, defies definition. Technically, poetry is writing which employs the verse line as a formal device. The format of a poem on paper looks different from prose. Prose generally conveys information and ideas. Poetry expresses emotions, although ideas are also involved.

The Complete Rhyming Dictionary defines poetry with an added dimension: "The expression of thoughts which awake the higher and nobler emotions or their opposites, in words arranged according to some accepted convention." That elevates it from a mere technical production to an art form.

Psalm 45:1 echoes Wordsworth's definition but directs it toward God. "My heart overflows with a good theme; I address my verses to the King; my tongue is the pen of a ready writer."

The terms *verse* and *poetry*, used loosely, refer to any work of a poet. I will use them interchangeably for all versified writing. The *Writer's Encyclopedia* states:

> Poetry is often used as a synonym for verse. Although all poetry may be considered verse—speech or writing in metrical form—not all verse may be thought of as poetry. The distinction between the two lies in the profundity of thought and emotion. For example, "Mary had a little lamb, its fleece was white as snow," is both lyrical and metrical; it does not, however, represent the depth of thought, imagination, and emotion that characterize poetry.

In a simple dictionary definition, *poetry* is "lofty thought or impassioned feeling expressed in imaginative words. *Verse* is any expression in words that conform to accepted metrical rules and structure."

The American poet, Clement Wood, maintained that the intellect can manufacture *verse* at any time because its technique is comparatively simple. Its meter, rhyme, alliteration, stanza arrangement and other devices may be mastered as easily as the multiplication tables. However, *poetry* comes differently, he claimed, from a deeper, basic source than thinking. Poetry comes from an inner compulsion, from compact desires and inspiration.

Identifiable mechanics of poetry

Certain recognizable elements of poetry distinguish it from prose. These help us recognize a poem when we meet one and guide us in our structure when we write one.

Line units. Sentences are not a characteristic of poetry. The jugular vein of poetry is the line.

Stanzas. These are successions of lines commonly bound together to form one of a series of similar groups. Stanzas must be repeated in order for us to recognize them as a pattern.

Strophe. Any separate section or extended movement in a poem is a strophe. We distinguish these from stanzas because they do not follow a regularly repeated pattern. Strophes are verse paragraphs or units of thought shown on the page by spaces between groups of lines or by initial indentation. The poet uses them to signal changes in thought or for effect.

Meter. A basic pattern of rhythm repeated throughout a poem, like the beat of music, represents meter. Poetry may or may not use a metrical pattern or rhyme to heighten its effectiveness.

Rhyme. The chiming of identical sounds of words gives us rhyme. Such words may occur within lines or at the end of lines.

White space. In a sense, white space is an element of poetry for visual effect. The use of white space also distinguishes poetry from prose. Although poetry is primarily an *auditory experience,* most people meet poems on paper. That is a good reason to make poetry a pleasing or interesting *visual experience* on the page. You may indent your lines to different degrees at intervals. You may vary your line length and shape your poem's lines into some recognizable design. You may stagger your lines in any innovative way you choose.

However, white space should be used and not abused. Avoid weird patterns of word or line spacing without good reason. Don't let lines dangle strangely unless you can justify doing so to enhance your purpose. Stanzas or strophes with spaces between them help the reader understand the flow of your poem, show a break in content, or surprise him with a twist of thought.

The idea. According to Michael J. Bugeja, writing in *The Art and Craft of Poetry,* the idea stands as the most important element of any poem. He says:

> Ideas unify our thoughts or feelings. They shape how we perceive the world and excite us with images of beauty or moments of truth. Since ancient times, poets have been known more for their ideas than for the words they used to convey them.

Am I a poet?

A poem is a personal expression *under the poet's complete control.* Judson Jerome put it this way:

> [When you write a poem], recognize that you are boss. You put what words in what form on the paper you please. There is no mysterious tribunal that decides that a piece of writing is or is not a poem. It is a poem if you call it one. I may choose not to publish it. I may not like it. But I have no right to say it is not a poem.

Therefore, for the purpose of this book, let's accept the premise that a poem is a poem if *you* say it is—whether it lacks technique and imagery, or is loaded with them. Let no one challenge you. Moreover, if you've written a poem, you can call yourself a poet.

Poetry as a recognized art form

I would, however, suggest a more precise and practical working definition. Burton Raffel, in *How to Read a Poem,* proposes: "Poetry is a (1) disciplined, compact verbal utterance, (2) in some more or less musical mode, (3) dealing with aspects of internal or external reality in some meaningful way." The first two elements are matters of craft. The third deals with the substance of the poem. Let's expand on that:

"Disciplined." Do not willy-nilly dash off lines from the top of your head and consider them poetry. Poetry is a craft you must skillfully work on until you round off and complete your poem. Balance, order and beauty of phrase do not just happen.

"Compact." Condense emotions and thoughts into a few lines that might otherwise take pages of prose to express. Economy of words characterizes poetry. Compress meaning into the fewest possible words.

"Verbal." Work and play with words, squeezing shades of meaning and nuances of expression from them. Try not to present them "plain vanilla."

"Utterance." Poetry should be spoken and heard, not only encountered on paper. Make your poem speak

to the ears of your reader through their eyes.

"*More or less musical mode.*" Employ some rhythm, not necessarily in a traditional meter, but through repetitions of words, phrases, expressions or use of white space. A poem can actually "sing" without musical notes. Poetry uses verbal music—good reason to read it aloud.

"*Dealing with aspects of internal reality.*" The poet looks within himself to listen to and examine his thoughts, feelings, senses, impressions and opinions. He draws them out and expresses them in words. He works to release the poet from within himself.

"*Dealing with aspects of external reality.*" The poet keenly observes life both in his immediate environment and the world at large. All human experiences are grist for reflection and scrutiny. The poet turns them into verbal expression.

"*In some meaningful way.*" Poetry must say something. Raffel maintains, "Mere beauty of phrase, mere intensity of musicality, mere ingeniousness of technique, become irrelevant in the absence of solid substance." Not only classic poetry but much contemporary poetry has acquired a special reputation for obscurity. Every poem needs to have a point which the reader should grasp without someone explaining it to him. That is different from having "a moral." We should not preach through a poem.

The amplified definition above puts your poem in a more serious light, doesn't it? We concede that you may call what you have written "a poem," and no one should contradict you. Nevertheless, we have a higher standard for our craft that demands more than quick inspiration.

As Christian writers of poetry, let us strive for excellence and present quality "verses to the King." When we minister to others through our poetry, let us do our personal best to express God's truth in beauty.

What is involved in being a poet?

All five senses come into play in the creation of a poem, but a poet's ears, eyes and heart are vital to writing poetry. Our *ears* hear and select the language we want to use to express sound. Not just a pleasing sound, but the precise sound to suit the thought. The poet instinctively feels and hears tone, rhythm and beat. An ear for poetry is partly inborn. Nevertheless, we can also acquire and improve it by reading poetry aloud and writing it.

As poets, we see the form our poem will take on paper, plan our lines, their length and composition, and arrange them for effect and dramatic appropriateness. Content, lines and strophes should come together for an overall purpose. Parallelism, variation, style and the importance of order and white space come into play—all visually perceived.

Poetry must have *heart*. Good poetry creates an emotional impact and aesthetic effect because it appeals to a reader's senses and passions. As such, poetry is an inward or introspective art form expressing strong feeling about something or someone. It is not simply the technical exercise of words on paper. Poets explore their intimate, inward and personal experiences and try to articulate them with intense attention.

Poetry is simply the most beautiful,
impressive, and widely effective mode of
saying things. Matthew Arnold.

Good poetry goes beyond expressing skillfully
what *the poet* feels. He must make *his reader* feel through
his poem. In his mind he must ask the reader, "Do you
see what I see? Do you hear what I hear? Do you feel,
smell, taste what I do?" The poet must invite the reader
into his experience.

The poet as a "creator"

Poetry is one creative art along with painting and
music. The writer's creative process is complex, vital and
exhilarating. As poets, we create because of an inward
urge—something we must do. We share this yearning to
express beauty and truth with painters, sculptors, musi-
cians and other artists. We love words and every aspect
of the creative writing process. We bring forth something
that has never existed. God created human beings in His,
the Creator's, image. We can't create in the same sense
that God created—out of nothing. Through our God-
given imagination, ideas and concepts, we combine our
impressions in word pictures. In that sense, writing a
poem is creating. We take what is inside of us or observed in life and share it with others through images,
sounds and rhythms.

Working hard to improve our craft of poetry should not take the enjoyment of our creation from us.

When God finished creating, He rested. He looked over what He had accomplished and said, "It is good!" Satisfaction and joy escalate when a more fulfilling, crafted poem takes shape from the first rough draft that emerged haltingly from its thought-shell. We, too, can exclaim, "It is good!" Not with self-centered pride, of course, but in honest appraisal and praise to the Creator who inspired it.

Three categories of poets

It may help us to think of three categories of poets or three pathways a poet can take. These are not fixed divisions—the line is often blurred between them.

(1) Joy writers. Most poets are in this category. They write for sheer delight and do not think about publication. They write for the joy and satisfaction of their creative expression, perhaps sharing their efforts with a small circle of family or friends.

(2) Freelancers. Joy writers may go beyond the first category and publish occasionally or regularly in newspapers, magazines and church or organizational publications. Prolific poets may publish their works in anthologies.

Some freelance poets look for markets that pay and then write poems specifically for them. They may write light verse or greeting card verse. Sometimes they write on assignment. Composers who write music lyrics may be in this category.

(3) *Professionals.* Usually secular writers, such poets publish in quarterlies and publications read by literary intellectuals. They publish books of poetry which those periodicals review. They seek recognition by other professionals and by the literary public. Even professional poets do not make their living through poetry, however. They sometimes support themselves through related vocations such as teaching, lecturing, editing or other forms of writing.

Can *anyone* become a poet?

When someone asked her that question, Luci Shaw, considered one of the premier poet/authors in the Christian world, replied:

> I think most people have an artistic impulse within themselves that can take different forms. Not everyone can be a composer or a painter. We can experiment with different media and different genres, but no, I don't think everyone is gifted to be a poet. Many people, however, have poetic gifts that haven't been developed.

"Just about everyone has more poetry *inside* than has yet come *outside*," writes poet and professor Elva McAllaster. "Despite potentialities," she continues, "the

thin ozone and craggy trails of poetry are *not* for everyone. If they prove to be your very habitat, congratula-
tions, and welcome!"

Let's receive that as an encouraging word and
follow the craggy trails up the steep mountain of writing
quality poetry.📖

A poem rarely "comes to you" full blown. The idea knocks on your mental door when you read an arresting phrase or hear a picturesque expression. Sometimes when you observe something intriguing or reflect on some aspect of life. Invite the idea in, entertain it awhile and decide where it is leading you.

3

Ideation in Poetry

> Although it turns upon the action of words, poetry roots in the acts of life. It springs from inner sources that are at the very core of our humanness—it resides in the interstices between the world and the unarticulated emotions circumscribing our souls. —Rita Dove

*T*he idea is only the first exciting step—afterward comes the hard work of crafting. Any subject or experience may provide a theme for a poem. You don't have to stick to the good old standbys of love or nature so characteristic of poetry. Being "in love" or responding to the awesomeness of nature does seem to evoke deep poetic feelings. Plato said, "Every man is a poet when he is in love." You can still write love poems with your fresh approach. Take an original, creative view of something in the natural world which makes it worthy of a poem and launch your idea.

In my second anthology, *Heaven and Nature Sing,* I compiled 50 of my poems describing God's creation from various perspectives. I wrote poems about what might be considered timeworn topics: clouds, each season, storm, color, fresh air, willow, fog, dandelion, first snowfall, the state of Virginia, gray days, lakes, rocks, a dead bird, grasshoppers, waterfall, mountains and light. Nevertheless, these were *my* responses and *my* feelings. Don't hesitate to write *your* fresh poems even on common subjects.

Poets through the ages and in all cultures must have written hundreds, thousands of poems about the season of spring. That should not stop me from writing another poem arising from my own emotions—nor should it stop you. I personified spring in the following poem:

Spring, the Lover

Spring startled me today
as I shook out the dust mop.
He took me by surprise
I didn't realize
he had arrived.
He slipped behind me
ruffled my hair with the wind
kissed my cheek with the sun
laughed to see me blush.
His warm breath caressed my neck
teasing me, making me restless
as I swept winter from the porch.

I tried to brush him from my mind
by staying indoors at humdrum tasks.
He rustled the curtains
flirting with me
through the open window.

I can't resist him!
I must run away with him
right away today. So I race
trowel and seeds in hand
to our garden rendezvous
our "special place"
eager for the touch
of the rich mulch
the sweet, earthy scent
of Virginia country soil.

Despite the lingering chill
of retreating March wind
I kneel in ecstasy
in the moist flower bed
breathing hard
delighted to feel basic nature
and the hope of life
incipient in the seed
about to experience
resurrection.

Basically, poetry expresses emotion. "My *heart overflows* with a good theme," (Psalm 45:1) describes intense feeling. Every nuance of any emotion provides an idea for a poem. As you reflect on your feelings toward anything in your natural environment, on your mental horizon or relating to your physical or spiritual life, you can make that emotion come alive in a poem by verbalizing, polishing and endowing it with similes and metaphors.

Much of my ideation for *prime time living* poems comes from having become a part of that age group and experiencing its joys and foibles. After many of those poems were published in magazines "for mature audiences," I compiled 118 of them into my first anthology, *Life—Stop Crowding Me!* Some of my ideas were: birthdays, loneliness, rocking chair, unfinished dreams, broken relationships, time running out, pruning, mortality, being dispensable, legacy, nostalgia, tears, pity party, old baggage, another chance, retirement, identity, empty nest, changes, pain, family problems and heritage roots.

As I thought about how much I still wanted to do and how little time was left, I wrote the following poem:

Lost Centerfold

I awoke one morning
to think about all the roads
I can't follow
because time is running out
all I can't do
because strength is failing.
I have begun
everything
but won't finish
anything.

Should I run and hide
from those dark thoughts?
Are they phantom fears?
How to separate
reality from fantasy
and not waste tears
on diminishing years?

What happened to middle age?
When I arrived
it wasn't there!
That isn't fair . . .
I leaped from young to old.
Where is the oversize centerfold
of prime time I counted on
to fulfill all my dreams?

The tomorrow I eagerly planned
vanished into the past tense
without the sense
of having lived it.
The face staring back at me
in the unflattering mirror
already did its living . . .
but when?
Where was I
when it happened?

In panic
I want to seize
a hammer and nail
and impale this moment
before it gets away

to stop the tick of the clock
because its rhythm
echoes my numbered heartbeat.
to restrain its hands
from advancing
to halt the sun
at blazing noonday
and keep away
lengthening shadows . . .
but I don't know how!

So I must endow *this moment*
with life and joy
and be bold
to make *today* my centerfold.
I dare not destroy
its intrinsic value
with the enticing decoy
of waiting for tomorrow
intending to borrow
by installments
each illusive day
to do my living.

Thank God for *now!*

I wrote other poems expressing a variety of
commonplace ideas: full schedule, pat answers, masks,
kitchen sanctuary, exercise, devotional life, trivial duties,
silence, spiritual depression, contentment, neighbors,
decision making, risk, wardrobe, crisis, monotony and
disappointments. I compiled these into my third anthology, *Songs of My Pilgrimage,* a potpourri of reflections on

my spiritual journey through the years.

For example, as a take-off on the Ephesians 6:10-18 passage, I wrote:

Designer Clothes

What shall I wear today, Lord?
I have a closet full of clothes
but I don't know what I'll face.
Shall I wear blue denim or lace?
What appointments lie ahead?
Where will I be led?

I just can't decide!
So, Lord, will You provide
and choose my outfit?
Whatever's in style and classy
will be all right with me . . .
I know I'll be a hit!

Oh, how well they go together:
matching hat and shoes
complementing accessories
the belt of truth
a sword to use!

(I can't say, however
that I'd select armor!
Something lighter
chic and trendy
even in haste
would have been
more to my taste.)

But You know best
what I will meet
in the marketplace
or on the street
that needs a shield
and sword and battle gear
out on the field
of my day.

I feel protected now
assured and guarded
come what may today.
I'll wear Your armor, Lord
more proudly than mink or sable
because the ensemble carries
Your designer label!

Each poem in my anthologies arose from a Christian world view, no matter how trivial the subject. You can treat any idea in different ways: humorously, seriously, religiously, for children, satirically or from the viewpoint of a different protagonist. You could develop the same idea or topic as a rhymed poem, in free verse, blank verse or any way your creative juices flow. Actually, there are no new ideas. Ideas are not copyrighted. Only your response to them and your creative development are unique. (See the author's book, *How to Capture and Develop Ideas for Writing.*)

I wrote poems about my impressions during travel and as I experienced life in other cultures. I traveled 14 times to the People's Republic of China since 1979, and my reflections on the lifestyle, struggles, political system, suffering of Christians and village life were ideas I tapped. I marketed them separately to magazines and then included some in my third anthology. I thought of ideas for poems when I encountered people and places in Israel and Egypt during another trip and compiled them in the same anthology.

Our tour group attempted to climb Mount Sinai during our trek from Egypt to Israel. Most of us became exhausted with the rugged terrain and failed to reach the summit. Later we visited Mount Calvary, so small by contrast. I compared the theological implications of the two locations:

Two Mounts

Sinai thunders "Do!"
Calvary whispers "Done!"

As Moses climbed Mt. Sinai
so I will try
sweating and straining
stumbling over jagged rocks
slipping on steep slopes
attempting Sinai's summit . . .
to make it only *half* way!

Sinai thunders "Do!"
The Law, given for the good of man
measures with a divine ruler
man's inability to attain
a "mission impossible" standard:
breaking one law
I stand condemned by all.

Calvary whispers "Done!"
Grace, bought by the blood of the One
who dragged a rugged cross
over rough cobblestones
up Calvary, instead of me
and made it *all* the way
to buy my freedom
from the perfect Law!

Sinai thunders "Do!"
Calvary whispers "Done
once for all!"

When I made the leap from my electric typewriter into the computer/word processing world, the awesome spiritual implications of the electronic technology almost overwhelmed me. I wrote 12 poems "for computer buffs who enjoy slipping disks" and published them in a chapbook under the title *Divine Applications.* I'm eager for some extended meditation time to express my feelings in another collection of poems since I have now bungee-corded off the *Internet* cliff into cyberspace. Anything can be an idea for a poem, as well as for any other genre of creative writing. Even the space bar on my computer keyboard gave me an idea for a poem:

Space Bar

I need to press the space bar:
my life is overcrowded.
I need better proportion
my words run together.

I'm too complicated
not communicating
what I am
or want to be
nor displaying accurately
God's life through me.

I want some distance
some intervals
between myself and others
not a gap or abyss
but accommodating elbowroom
perhaps headroom
away from distractions.
I need space to sort out
where I am going
and where I've been
a comfortable interim
to look within.

Then I can go on.
A space is not a period
a finality, or a full stop
only a pausing place
an interlude
to open up the words of my life
so I can decide more wisely
what I want to say
and where I want to be.

You might explore the *monologue* or *dialogue* format of writing a poem. In a monologue not only the poet
speaks but his thoughts are revealed. I imagined conversa-

tions with God in many of my poems, as David and others did in some of the Psalms.

I pose a question in my heart, perhaps a struggle, and express it to God in a prayer. Then I imagine God's response to my dilemma, being careful to stick to biblical principles and truth, of course. We should never take liberties by putting words that are not Scriptural into the mouth of God. Prayer poems are among the most beautiful and meaningful themes for Christian poets.

From Psalm 90:12, "Teach us to number our days and recognize how few they are; help us to spend them as we should," I set the following poem in dialogue:

My Request

"God, I demand a large easel
on which to paint all my ambitions
a durable canvas
a spacious studio
quality oil paints
a complete spectrum of colors
and plenty of time
to accomplish my life masterpiece."

Instead . . .
God gave me a fragile easel
a petite palette of primary water colors
confined me to a cramped room
without the guarantee
of threescore and ten years
in which to emblazon my dreams
on a miniature, disposable canvas.

"That isn't fair, God!" I complained.

My Beloved Son, in only 33 years
in an obscure corner
of an oppressed land
among hostile people
and misunderstanding friends
without media blitz
reconciled heaven and earth
interpreted eternity to man
and declared, "It Is Finished!"

I fell as God's feet
ashamed of my audacity.
"Your Majesty! Lord of my days!
Accept my praise
for whatever You grant me.
Help me understand
Your perfect plan
for mortal man
and for me.
Show me how to accept
joyfully and soberly
both limitation and opportunity.
Teach me to number my days
that I may apply my heart
unto wisdom and learn
to paint by their number."

Who's talking?

Persona (the Latin word for person) is the narrating presence, the voice, in the poem—a literary pose. The persona can be either the poet himself—you—or a character you assume, perhaps a mask you wear, as in a drama. Burton Raffel, in *How to Read a Poem,* maintains that a poem does not require authentic autobiography, particularity or history. A poem may be about emotions without being about actual people who experienced those emotions.

You don't need to limit yourself to writing a poem about your own experience or from a personal viewpoint. You may use your creative imagination to express plausible feelings of someone else or thoughts you may or may not think. You may use personification and write from the perspective of a river, an inanimate object, or a season. With various personae you can develop unlimited ideas. I wrote from the viewpoint of a piece of driftwood in the following:

Driftwood

I am driftwood
tossed upon an uncaring sea
pitched about by circumstance
bobbing aimlessly
hurled from side to side
with the tide
yet an eternal force
drew me as by a magnet
cast me at last
upon an unfriendly shore.

Drifting no more
unnoticed I lay

beneath the scorching sun
and blistering sky
until . . .
Loving Hands rescued me
caressed my coarseness
saw my potentiality
and dreamed a dream
for me.

Cleaned and polished now
by Caring Hands
I am redeemed, reclaimed
fashioned to a work of art
by Skillful Hands
Nail-pierced Hands
and I am no longer
simply driftwood.

*Y*ou are free to decide the format for your poem. You may choose a ready-made box (traditional format) or climb on top of all the boxes and express yourself as you please. You don't have to squeeze yourself into anyone else's style.

4

Poetry Formats

The form of your poem is like a trellis which provides structure and stability to your poem—the vine with blossoms that climbs on it. Both form and content are important.

*Y*ou may give your poem whatever form you wish. You may want to write poems in traditional classic patterns or develop your own form, one in which you are comfortable. You may name it after yourself, if you wish. Poets Homer and Robert Burns did both—sometimes they followed ready-made forms, other times they created their own patterns. So can you. If you aim for publication, what your desired market usually accepts is what form you might choose.

The thought or emotion you want to convey in a poem may dictate the format. Be adventuresome and creative. Experiment with different forms and fresh approaches.

Why should a Christian poet bother to learn traditional forms of poetry? Why not just do his own thing, since "a poem is a poem." The poet, like a carpenter, must first master the elements of his craft with a thorough understanding of meter, rhyme, stanza, structure, metaphor, connotation and tone. Lacking that competence, the poet may produce shoddy writing without meaningful form. His work will lack the power to memorably bring forth an illuminating idea or emotion worthy of "verses for the King."

The choice is yours

You will find details and examples on the use of forms and patterns in any book on the craft of poetry. Several excellent texts are listed later. I will comment on only two of the major forms.

(1) *Traditional rhymed.* One market with which most of us are familiar, though it is becoming less and less popular, is the traditional, strictly rhymed and metered form. The poems of Helen Steiner Rice are a good example. Her poems on greeting cards, gift booklets and books market well to a select audience. But if you plan to write and market that type of poetry, your audience is diminishing.

Most people think of a poem as rhymed. However, rhyme did not come first as a characteristic of English poetry.

Rhyme didn't become popular until the late 14th century and was rarely used before the Norman Conquest in 1066. Prior to that, blank verse with regular meter or beat distinguished English poetry.

Judson Jerome pointed out in his poetry column in *Writers Digest,* "The reason for the prejudice *against* rhyme is that so many amateur poets use it badly. In the first place, they have not mastered meter, and nothing so pains the ear as a rhyme achieved by the wrenching of meter. If you rhyme at all, find fresh rhymes and ... use them in places other than at the end of lines."

You seldom find strictly rhymed poetry in literary magazines, although it still appears in religious and inspirational magazines. Editors of religious publications, however, seem to accept fewer traditional poems in favor of free verse. Nevertheless, if your poet within feels more comfortable writing conventional rhymed and metered poetry, you are certainly free to do so. Be sure, however, that you write quality verse for the King. Hymn writers of the last few centuries wrote the lyrics of great hymns in traditional form. They continue to move the hearts of Christians in succeeding generations.

A delightful exception!

For those whose gift is writing for children, rhyme and rhythm is the way to go. Children have natural rhythm—they love to be rocked and instinctively swing and sway. Early in life they experiment with new language skills by imitating the sound of rhymes. They respond to the singsong of a regular beat. They easily remember end-rhymes in nursery poems. Their first story books and poems should be full of basic rhyme. A child's first prayer and first blessing at mealtime is usually rhymed. Children want to hear rhymed poems over and over even before they learn to read.

Writing for children is a special skill which not all of us have. Rhymed poetry can be an enchanting challenge for the Christian poet and a special ministry to little ears.

(2) *Free verse.*

Try your wings by writing free verse—the most popular form of poetry today and the most versatile. In free verse you are the only one to decide when and where to break a line, make a stanza and end a poem. Basically, you can write whatever and however you want. To some, this style may not seem to be *real* poetry. There is no right or wrong way to write free verse—that would be a contradiction of terms.

Walt Whitman is widely acknowledged as the founding father of free verse, one of the first poets to popularize this style. He caused a sensation in his day by writing poetry with uneven lines.

In free verse, the length of lines is not measured by a specific number of units. It builds on cadence, images and a delicate sense of balance, not necessarily on any recurring beat. The unit in free verse is not the foot, as in metrical verse, but the *strophe*, which is defined as a unit of thought. The line of free verse is based on words in natural stress groupings.

The line sometimes ends where a pause or falling inflection of voice would naturally come while reading or speaking. But not necessarily. Where to break a line is not easy to decide. Most poets employ instinct. They have no fixed standard but seem to divide lines whenever they feel the urge. The poet may break lines after significant words or thoughts or start each new line with significant words.

End-stopped free verse makes a line break at the point of a natural pause. Such lines are usually longer. *Run-on* or *enjambed* free verse breaks lines where there is no grammatical or syntactical pause. Sometimes the line unexpectedly breaks between adjectives and nouns or in the middle of a natural phrase. Sometimes at a point of suspense. Lines are usually shorter in enjambed free verse. The poet can slow and speed the reader's pace with line breaks.

A free verse line sometimes ends on a strong word, and the next line starts with an unstressed syllable and leads through the next grouping of words, which, by their meaning and association, belong together. A sense of balance in free verse is important. Watch for awkward or weak lines and rework them.

Contrary to what the reader of free verse might think, it is not easy to write quality free verse. A poet must introduce his idea, develop the message and then conclude, as in metrical poetry, with his strongest point or a surprise.

Without some degree of figurative language in free verse, you may as well write in prose. Arranging a page in lines of varying length does not justify calling the result a poem.

Free verse is definitely not simply chopping up little thoughts into dangling phrases dribbling artistically down a page. On the other hand, I've read some tremendous prose saturated with poetic expressions, alliteration, metaphors and similes. I've had to restrain myself from running to my word processor and typing the prose in line units. I am sure we would consider the result to be poetry.

As an example, when I read the first paragraph of a prose article by C.D.Wright, *The Choice For Poetry*, in *The Writer* magazine, I did just that—I typed it in free verse lines, using every word of the writer's prose. To me, the prose tasted delightfully like poetry.

Always Arkansas

Every year
the poem I most want to write
changes shapes,
changes directions.
It refuses to come forward
to stand still
while I move to meet it
to embrace it, to coax it
to sit on the porch with me
and watch the lightning bugs steal
behind the fog's heavy veil,
listen for the drag of john boats
through the orchestra of locusts and frogs.
An old hand-plow supports the mailbox,
a split-rail fence borders the front lot.

Hollyhocks and sunflowers loom there.
At the end of the lot, the road forks off
to the left, toward the river
and then to the right
toward the old chicken slaughterhouse.
The poem hangs back, wraithlike
yet impenetrable as briar.
The porch is more impressive
than the rest of the house.
A moth as big as a girl's hand
spreads itself out on the screen door.
The house smells like beets.
For in this poem
it is always Arkansas
summer, evening.
But in truth, the poem never sleeps
unless I do,
for if I were to come upon it
sleeping, I would net it.
And that would be that—
my splendid catch.

Can free verse ever rhyme? Who is to say it can't?
Much does. Rhyme is not a crime! Rhyme never saved a
bad verse nor spoiled a good one. Most of the world's
poetry is unrhymed, including most of the best poetry in
our European, Western tradition. Alliteration, consonance
or any verbal harmony is a kind of rhyme. An accomplished poet can rhyme or not as he pleases, and the
result is quality poetry.

Can free verse be metrical? Of course. Most of it can be scanned by some conventional techniques. Rhythm provides a background pattern and gratifies the reader with harmony. On the other hand, poor rhythm can stop or confuse him with dissonance. Rhythm gives shape and organization. Sound and not spelling determines rhyme. Much of the best rhyming is internal, subtle, occurring in the middle of phrases and within lines.

The point is not whether the poet does or does not like rhyme. The decision to rhyme or not to rhyme depends entirely on what he wants to accomplish with the poem.

Do poetic words make a poem? In the matter of *diction*, no word is inherently more poetic than any other, i.e., nightingales, moon, June, sighs, hearts, sable locks, languish, ere, 'twill, lo, blithe or methinks. Poets tend to overwork such words and their use characterizes an amateur. When writing poetry today, whether you rhyme or not, avoid *poeticism*—using fancy language with the intention of making it sound poetic. Today's poets are advised to avoid "other worldly" words and *King James* language such as "thees" and "thous." However, if *your* poet within wants to do so in a prayer poem as "a verse for the King," who dares to challenge him?

To all the above questions about free
verse, there is still only one answer, one
that is sometimes difficult to believe and
understand: *free verse has no rules!*

Robert Frost said, "Writing free verse is like playing tennis with the net down." Frost didn't care much for
free verse. Judson Jerome carried the simile one step
further and approached it more positively. He said it is
not only like playing without a net, but without a court,
rackets, balls or a partner. The player is free, of course, to
use any or all of those familiar elements he wishes. But he
can dispense with one and all, and, Jerome maintains, if he
chooses to, he can still call the game "tennis."

Every line of poetry should be interesting for *the
way it speaks* as well as for *what it says.* Writing free verse
forces you to exert new pressures on the language, to
twist the lines tighter, to discover new relationships
between words. Free verse challenges you to find more
evocative and fresh images and diction. It requires you to
arrange words on the page so the pattern itself will have
meaning, as in the echo of beginning words at the end.

As a poet, you might experiment with many
forms—classic, fixed, recognizable patterns and your own
style. Your practice in one mode supports and deepens
your practice and skill in others. *After* you learn the disci-

pline of structured poetry, you can continue to the delightful emancipation of free verse.

I prefer writing free verse. I use rhyme if it feels right, if it falls into place naturally. Or I rhyme at random. I may rhyme within lines or not at all, if it doesn't enhance my poem. I try to paint naturally with words using similes, metaphors and alliteration if it doesn't sound contrived. I prefer to repeat sounds within phrases or stanzas rather than use end-rhymes. I have found my own way and feel comfortable. I don't have to defend my style to anyone because it works for me. You, too, are free to find your own way as you write poetry.

How do you know if you have *style?*

Joseph D. Adams, noted poet, professor, writer and artist, commented on style:

No one effectively teaches "style" in a creative writing class. The reason is simple. Style is too amorphous to describe, difficult to engineer, and almost impossible to change. Everyone who writes has style, whether he is aware of it or not. Consequently, it's incorrect to talk about an absence of style. When one denigrates a person's style, one is actually attacking the way that person presents himself.

Consider, for example, several top artists. Let's say, Walt Whitman, Robert Frost, and E.A. Robinson. When we dip into their works and familiarize ourselves with their way of addressing us, we can no longer confuse one with the other. Why? The simple answer—their styles are very different.

Adams explains that style is the sum of the poet's presentation, including the writer's voice, diction, predilection for certain subject matter, attitudes or tones, and preference for certain genres or presentation schemes. "If we don't like a person's style," Adams states, "we might be inclined to call the style bad. On the other hand, we may disagree with a person's content, yet add, 'I like his or her style.'"

Basically then, *style is you*. It comes from your poet within. You may find yourself naturally falling into a certain style, although you can't consciously identify it. The poet within you asserts himself in his familiar way each time you express an idea for a poem. However, you may find it creative and refreshing to switch between various modes, forms and approaches and stretch yourself within your craft. It's not necessary to lock into a single style.

As you exercise your poetic gift and craft, you find your direction, the format that suits you best, your most comfortable structure. You don't have to defend it to anyone. Relax and experience joy and excitement in your poetic journey! *Release the poet within you to do unexpected things!* 📖

*E*very art form has its
particular characteristics.
Figures of speech, picturesque
language and poetic devices
identify poetry. These add color,
vividness and freshness to
versification.

5

Figures of Speech and Poetic Devices

Since poetry appeals to word lovers, figures of speech add interest, generate excitement and fire the imagination. The English language has rich resources for us to tap.

*T*oday's readers and markets look for crisp writing with sparkle, poems that sing and stir the emotions, poems that show, not just tell.

The *Writer's Encyclopedia* defines figures of speech as techniques that furnish the writer with a nonliteral means of conveying images. Included in such figures are hyperbole, irony, metaphor, metonymy, onomatopoeia, paradox, imitation, personification and simile. Let's review a few that are commonly used in poetry.

A *simile* compares or relates two similar things to

each other, generally using either the word *like* or *as*. Try to replace tired similes like "fresh as a daisy" or "white as snow" with more creative ones. Keep to similes familiar to the reader, however. The "Picturesque Speech" page of the *Reader's Digest* should challenge the poet to try more descriptive expressions.

Metaphor compares unlike objects or ideas. The writer declares that something *is* or *was* something else, not similar to it. An example: "The Lord is my light. . . ." The words *like* or *as* are not used. Be consistent by using the same metaphor throughout your poem. Try to give fresh treatment to overused metaphors.

Personification attributes human form, characteristics or sensibilities to inanimate objects, animals or ideas. The Bible abounds with examples like "trees clap their hands."

Imitation has a cousin called *parody*. Sometimes a poet deliberately imitates the work of another, not to plagiarize, but as a takeoff on some existing form or structure. Parody is a humorous or satirical imitation of a serious piece of literature, musical composition, person or event. As an example, poets have given Samuel Clement's *'Twas the Night Before Christmas* many a twist through the years, sometimes humorous, other times serious.

Onomatopoeia can be used with skill to add vividness to poetic descriptions. It is a word whose sound represents or vocally imitates a physical sound associated it. Plop, click sizzle, buzz are examples.

Other poetic devices

Poetic devices delight the ear and the eye of the reader. They enhance appreciation of poetry as an art form.

Alliteration is the use of words beginning with the same consonant or letter or having the same or similar sound. It played a strong role in Old English verse, and poets continue to use it generously. I have used alliteration liberally in the following poem as well as onomatopoeia, personification, metaphors and similes:

Winter in My Valley

The wind whines in a minor key
blowing icy breath
through cracks in our doors
feeling with frigid fingers
for gaps beneath window sills.
The gust heralds a blizzard that lurks
in the somber gray stretch of sky
advancing with threatening certainty.

As if to toll a frantic warning bell
the wind tugs at oak tops
and shakes the nearly naked branches
showering the ground
with a flurry of faded leaves.

Sniffing the scent of winter
small creatures scurry
furtively preparing shelters

vying with burrowing insects
to stockpile their larders
in the seasonal struggle for survival
while pond-life retreats to deepest waters
putting vital signs "on hold" till spring.

Sudden dusk descends on The Valley.
Hush settles over the silhouetted landscape
the gusty gale subsides
its announcement dispatched.
The first few flakes of snow soon merge
into sifting, swirling powdered sugar
swiftly frosting peaks of pointed frozen grass
into stiff meringue on neighboring field and hill
until a silver coverlet obliterates the familiar.

Accept my invitation, friend
to welcome the appointed storm
by enjoying the polar panorama
before the warmth of my crackling hearth.
Join me in retreat behind Jack-Frost windows
to contemplate the outdoor bluster
in snug pleasure and the treasure
of good company as we toast our toes
and drink a toast to the impending snow.
Let us celebrate the cycle of seasons
and winter's measured approach
in the Shenandoah Valley.

Repetition or refrain can be a single word, a phrase,
a sound or a whole line. If these are repeated at some
regular or irregular intervals in a poem, they become a
refrain. Repetition can be a form of emphasis. We usually
refer to stanzas in hymns as refrains.

Rhyme, as I have already pointed out, usually means the sound of words with the same vowel sounds or end consonants or combination of consonants. Spelling does not determine rhyme; the sound does. Rhyme can occur at other points in a poem than at the ends of lines. If inner rhyme follows a pattern, occurring in the same place in two or more lines, we call it *internal rhyme*. If it occurs randomly, it is called *slant rhyme*. Rhyme combines with meter to add melody to a beat, enhances the meaning of a poem and sets the mood for the content. In my example poem above, I use many internal and slant rhymes.

Poets debate the advisability of using a rhyming dictionary. Michael J. Bugeja, in *The Art and Craft of Poetry*, suggests that a rhyming dictionary may become a crutch and damage the creative process. The poet tends to concentrate too much on rhyming and not enough on the overall purpose of the poem and ideas he wants to convey.

Don't let the rhyming dictionary dictate
your next thought—stay in charge, or
you will end up writing nonsense.

Many experienced poets systematically go through the alphabet in their minds to explore possible rhymes. If you use a rhyming dictionary wisely and remain in control of your writing process, you will be using it appropriately.

Meter or rhythm

Meter is the poetic measure or arrangement of words in rhythmic lines or verses. The English language has a natural rhythm or cadence. Meter is a *regular* rhythm or sound to which you can tap your feet, like the beat of music. Meter is also accentual-syllabic rhythm, a sound that takes into account the number of accents (or hard stresses) along with the number of syllables in each line.

Consult any book on the craft of poetry for a more technical treatment of common meters, their names and examples. The following will refresh your memory with a few basic terms:

An *iamb* is a two-syllable word, (or two one-syllable words) one unaccented syllable and one accented—a light/hard stress. The inflection is on the last syllable, as in "toDAY." Each iamb or pair of light and hard syllables is called a *foot. Pentameter* refers to five pairs of such sounds, or five feet. Ninety percent of English verse is *iambic pentameter,* a line with five iambs. Example: I think/you want/to write/the best/you can.

Blank verse is simply unrhymed verse. Any line pattern, if unrhymed, is blank verse. Heroic blank verse is unrhymed iambic pentameter. We find it in drama, narrative and longer reflective poems, for example, in most of the writings of Shakespeare. Many consider pentameter to be the most neutral and flexible form for all poetic purposes.

You can scan poetry written in meter. *Scan* means to analyze a poem to detect its meter or beat. When you read a line of poetry aloud a number of times you will feel or sense a rhythm. Some of the types of sounds, the primary combinations of light and hard stresses that make up accentual-syllabic meter, are iamb, trochee, anapest and dactyl. (Again, consult poetry craft books for examples.)

Don't get lost in the mechanical process of writing poems. As you focus your creative powers on fashioning a poem, you should enjoy yourself. Let the idea flow naturally from your poet within.

Play with words, forms, images and figurative expressions. Your poem will never be "perfect," (whatever that would mean) but it will be *yours*. The more you write, the more you will probably develop a distinctive style of your own.

*J*esus spoke of going into one's closet—to a secret, private place—to pray. The poet who is a Christian should not be shy and keep his writing hidden in that prayer closet. He should emerge ebullient with inspiration and ideation to write for the glory of God.

6

The Poetry Writing Process

Donald Hall, a contemporary poet, admits that the most exciting thing is when you don't know where a poem is coming from. "The beginning words or lines come to you heavy and freighted with feeling, covered with signs saying, 'Pay attention to this. This is important.' But you don't know why."

riting poetry demands some measure of a reflective life. We need intervals when our souls can be quiet. However, there is so much background noise in our culture that it saps our energy and stifles our creativity. We live in a TV-shaped world where silence seems threatening, and even if we seek it, illusive. We suffer from that loss of silence. We must listen in silence and then speak and write out of it. It is God's natural rhythm, as Ecclesiastes observes, "a time to be silent and a time to speak."

Most of us can't ditch our jobs and families to follow some phony artistic lifestyle, and "ivory towers" are too high-priced to rent. We need to cultivate small patches of silence in our daily lives so our outer person can be calm and the inner one truly spontaneous. David Kirby reminds us, "Poems are not found on the surface of life. The poet must dive deeply for them." We must work toward some semblance of an orderly life with a generous measure of self-discipline.

The poet shouldn't try to escape from the "real" world. That world is the one from which his ideas spring and where the audience lives for whom he writes. Those to whom the Christian poet wants to minister live in the everyday world, and he needs to rub shoulders with them. Jesus prayed for His disciples, and for us at long range, "I do not ask Thee to take them out of the world, but ... sanctify them in the truth. Thy word is truth" (John 17:15,17).

Do you have a confining job, a harried household, perhaps a limited lifestyle of some sort? The apostle Paul did his best writing under unimaginable hardship and suffering in prison and during on-the-run missionary travel.

Judson Jerome wrote, "You do not become a poet as one becomes a doctor, lawyer or businessman. One becomes a doctor, lawyer or businessman, and, when he can, writes poetry." Terry Anderson, the Associated Press reporter held hostage in Lebanon for six years, wrote poems in his head during his imprisonment because he wasn't allowed pencil and paper. He recited them in his head daily, and during the first hour of his release wrote down eleven of his poems.

Dana Gioia, during his busy career as a vice-president of Kraft General Foods, wrote poems and essays for publications like *The New Yorker* and *The Atlantic*. He jotted down momentary flashes of inspiration so they wouldn't get lost. Writing in a journal, he said, keeps his imagination open to stimuli and helps focus his mental energy in a creative manner.

Because ideas for poems can strike at any moment, keeping a journal is one of the most helpful idea gleaners. In the midst of your active life, whatever it is, you can record the unexpected visits of the poet within. Every poet should have more ideas for poems than he has time to compose. Always have poems in progress to work on during your patches of silence.

Start with *brain spill* or *heart spill*

Everyone crafts a poem uniquely. *The Complete Rhyming Dictionary*, edited by Clement Wood, suggests, "A wise procedure for the poet is to write down what comes, as it comes, even if only a single line or less is the result. As far as possible, write out the poem without delay, to prevent [it being silenced forever]."

A good recommendation! Write while your poetic juices are flowing and put your rough thoughts or *brain spill* on paper. *Heart spill* is emotional expression, letting your feelings hang out.

Since a poem is basically "born" or "created," don't worry about how it arrives on the delivery table—there is no right or wrong way to compose a poem. Let your poet within decide how he is birthed.

I believe that what I have to say is more important than the form, but the form seems to take shape naturally as I write and usually surprises me. Often a first line comes to me as my starting gun. One book on poetry described that sparkling first line or phrase as a "zinger." After that comes the sweaty effort of *sprinting* to a rough draft. Hard work but fun!

Give your poem time to develop. It may come in pieces over a period of time. Let a potential beginning dangle loose for awhile. Be patient if the middle appears first, or if the end, the clincher, the punch line, arrives first. My practice is to write down on a yellow legal pad, in my almost illegible handwriting, all the quick thoughts and random words and phrases that come tumbling out. But if I don't get to my word processor rather soon to transcribe my *brain spill,* I can't decipher my scribbling later!

Sometimes a picturesque phrase or thought-provoking idea from some other piece of writing leaps out to become the nucleus of my poem. Usually I don't know where I will go with it, but I enjoy the discovery of the uncertain journey. I'm delighted when I arrive at something in black and white that seems to have promise. I don't outline my thoughts, although some poets do. My own ending usually surprises me. I don't often use my rhyming dictionary, instead, I let my rhymes happen more or less as they wish. I favor internal rather than end-rhymes.

Every poet has his own way of dealing with *brain spill* and *heart spill* while working on drafts. We can't exactly imitate each other's method of writing because each inner muse is unique. But we can help one another by sharing suggestions that seem to work. Go with whatever works for *you*.

Stay in kindergarten?

What attitude should a *beginning* poet bring to the exacting field of writing quality poetry, if he wants to minister to people and also have the marketplace look favorably on his work? And how should the *more advanced* Christian poet approach his craft?

In *The Writer* magazine, C.D. Wright, a publisher and university professor with six collections of poetry to his credit, advised:

> In this calling—which is more spiritual than material—it is imperative to *stay a beginner*. In other callings, this status would render you dysfunctional. You would be going, as they say, nowhere. Nevertheless, I resist the word *amateur* being applied to the word *poet*. I feel even more strongly about the term *professional*.

To "stay a beginner" does not mean we should be satisfied in a juvenile comfort zone, produce mediocre work and not bother trying to improve our craft. We should never reach the point where we cease studying and imitating great poets, honing our skills and cultivating the embryo gift God has given us. "Stir up the gift that is within you," as the apostle Paul advised Timothy. If writing poetry is one of your gifts from God, be a responsible steward to develop it.

Wright's point is that we should maintain a *beginner's attitude* in the sense of an innocent, childlike approach and pristine appreciation of all that comprises life. Our five senses must continue to be keen and sensitive. We should think and feel as if we were encountering a thought or emotion for the first time. When we reflect on an idea with freshness, hopefully we will craft it into a poem of depth and originality.

Robert Mezey wrote, "Think what Emily Dickinson managed to live without—sex, travel, drugs, a career—and yet few Americans have ever lived as fully, as intensely as she. Live your life. One cannot write out of books."

Live, experience, observe, reflect. It is not necessary that your experience be wide, only that it be deep.

What form of poetry will work best for you?

David Kirby writes, "Poetry changes. A hundred years ago, formal poetry dominated the scene. Then free verse came along. And now new free-verse forms appear every day. That doesn't mean that formal poetry has disappeared; to the contrary, formal poets are inventing new poem-types of their own."

Experiment. Probe your own skills as you try conventional, metered forms. Then stretch to explore free verse. Go off the charts, if you wish, and invent your own style. But Robert Mezey cautions, "Before you break the rules, you need to know the rules; before you seek novelty, you ought to demonstrate that you know the ancient craft."

The verses in Isaiah 54:2-3 may apply: "Enlarge the place of your tent; stretch out the curtains of your dwellings, spare not; lengthen your cords, and strengthen your pegs. For you will spread abroad to the right and to the left. . . ."

"Spare not." Don't limit your horizon! You may find that more than one form fits your talent. You may spread *both* to the right *and* to the left. However, it is essential to "strengthen your pegs," to work on the techniques of your craft so the wind of rejections and adverse circumstances won't blow away your tent. Stay open to how the Lord might want to stretch your poetry into new avenues of ministry.

David Kirby wrote, "Poems are happiest in the company of other poems, so don't try to create them in a vacuum. You probably wouldn't try to write four novels at once, but there's no reason why you shouldn't take advantage of poetry's brevity and get several poems going simultaneously."

As part of the stretching process, most published and prolific poets recommend working on several poems at once. Your poet within doesn't like to be rushed. He is a leisurely muse. Draw him out a little, listen to him intently and hear what he wants to say. Some poems may never go anywhere, they just wanted to play around with words awhile. If you work on other poems at the same time, you won't be frustrated if some simply refuse to fly.

Take your poem to surgery

I discuss marketing in the next chapter. However, never hurry your poetry to publication. Many well-known poets wrote for many years experimenting with their craft, learning the basics, developing ideas, discovering what worked best to draw out their poet within. They did endless revising before they ever sent a poem to an editor.

Both too early rejection and too early acceptance may be damaging to your future poetic health.

When and if the time comes to market your poetry, *be sure your poem is as good as you can possibly make it.* Editors want and hope to receive good writing, including quality poems. If your prose writing needs some help, an editor can cut, slant and otherwise edit it to his specifications. *But he won't perform surgery on your poem.* Since the owner of an art gallery can't retouch a painting, an editor doesn't have the right to alter your poem. Not because it is perfect, but because that just isn't done with poetry as an art form.

Therefore, be sure you edit it carefully yourself before you send it. It didn't drop from heaven as a flawless gem. Set aside your ego. Don't think of your poem as your unblemished child who can't be improved upon. To a certain extent, repair work can even be done on a baby or growing child for bow legs, cleft palate, crooked teeth, birthmarks or poor eyesight. Likewise you can improve your poem. Don't think of your poem more highly than you ought to think, especially in its infant and developing stages.

One widely published poet declared that his poems required a number of drafts—perhaps twenty, maybe fifty! Don't be discouraged. Do your personal best, but recognize that your first thought is *not* necessarily the best thought. In fact, first thoughts tend to be banal, not focused, conventional, not quite coherent. Revise your poem brutally and repeatedly before submission. Don't pack it off to market too soon.

Don't be too easily satisfied. Precision, liveliness and an air of spontaneity are the fruit of long hours of writing and rewriting, of trial and error.

Let any poem cool for a considerable time after you create it. Let it *season* and then focus on it with new eyes and an objective, critical attitude. You should especially want to revise and improve a poem you wrote some time ago because *you* are changing, growing, maturing and gaining more experience and skill.

I revise every poem I've written or published at least once more whenever I bring it to the display screen of my word processor or see it in print. (During the final, perhaps twentieth editing of this book, I brutally revised every poem of mine that I included as an example—I cut words, dropped phrases, substituted better thoughts and expressions, corrected the continuity and weeded out unnecessary punctuation. And I'll do it again before the next printing.)

Even after your poem is published, it is not set in concrete. Your poem is still in process because you are. Edit it again.

If your poem comes back from an editor, improve it at least once more before you submit it elsewhere. Don't overwork all the vitality out of your poem, however. At some point you must stop revising, shut your eyes and courageously release it.

Please look at my poem

To whom should you show your poetry if you want an honest evaluation? Sorry, but you usually can't trust comments from family and friends since they are understandably biased for (or against!) you. They may either overreact or fail to respond sensitively to a poem because they know, or *think* they know you.

Should you ask other poets to evaluate your work? Most poets can benefit from helpful suggestions of other poets and from poetry writers' workshops. However, sometimes poets are more reluctant or sensitive about accepting help from their peers than are writers of other genres. Poetry seems so personal, so subjective. Typically, although we may not want to admit it, we poets seek appreciation and validation more than critical help, even though the latter would probably be more valuable.

When a poet asks for suggestions about his poem, what he may really be asking for is a "brief shower of admiration!" Let's generously but honestly offer that to each other. Then, if we really must "rain on his parade" with at least a few raindrops, (constructive suggestions) our initial affirmation will serve as an umbrella. Always find some specific things in a fellow poet's work that you can genuinely applaud.

The value of workshops

Workshops, formal or informal, can take place anywhere: creative writing programs at universities, meetings in community centers, writers' gatherings in homes, groups in schools and at conference sites— anywhere writers meet each other. Poetry societies often sponsor workshops. They tend not to be large groups because everyone is expected to participate. Experienced poets or teachers usually lead and set the goals and format of the gatherings.

Poets involved in workshops commit themselves to improve their work by submitting poems for critique sessions. Some workshop goals are: to hone one's style, try new formats, garner more ideas, learn how to in- crease productivity and do better marketing. Workshops are a fairly recent model. Poets of the past usually worked alone, perhaps interacting with only one or two poet friends.

In workshops at writers' conferences, participants are often expected to compose new poems on immedi- ate assignment from the leader. The leader and group members critique each other's writing for mutual benefit.

It is important to compete only with yourself, not attack other poets whose style or ideas differ from yours. Nor should you be defensive about your poem when it is exposed on the table for surgery. Sometimes workshops include the discussion of selected contemporary and/or classical poems. The leader often makes himself available for one-on-one appointments for critiquing.

Ruth E. McDaniel advises, "Don't take criticism personally. Develop a thick hide and a proper perspective. Face it! Not everyone is going to love your style of poetry. Poetry is very selective, and you need good common sense to weed out positive criticism from personal bias."

Not everyone benefits from workshops, however. Because writing poetry is largely a solitary and deeply personal matter, some poets don't care to write in public or even resist writing an assigned poem as an "on the spot" exercise within a given time frame. Producing on demand, as it were, may not be the way their personal muse writes. It is not a matter of ego—their ideation and inspiration simply come in other ways. Their poet within doesn't require priming but prefers to express what is already there. Not all poets search for topics to write about. Some inner muses have more ideas than they will write in a lifetime.

This is not a criticism of the workshop idea, but a recognition of its limitations and the need to allow for differences in personal writing habits. Workshops are not a "one size fits all" panacea. Moreover, if the workshop isn't exclusively for poets but includes prose writers, perhaps in the majority, the benefit to participating poets may be diminished.

On the other hand, some beginning poets gain immeasurably from workshop interaction. They discover that they are not alone in their craft, and may form lasting, mutually beneficial friendships with some of their poet peers. Workshops force them to write and may help them overcome writing blocks. Some poets thrive on group stimulation, and learn to put aside their egos and rewrite when suggestions are offered.

As a workshop participant, you need to be sure of yourself as a writer otherwise your self-confidence may be shaken. A lot depends on how the leader handles sensitive criticism among the group. Each poet should remain open to suggestions for improvement, but still evaluate recommendations carefully. The poem is yours and it was begotten from your poet within. Accept constructive advice, if it enhances what *you* want to express. You are the only judge of that.

*T*o increase the chance of an
editor accepting your poetry,
approach your final editing
objectively and with a clear head.
Inspiration time is over—now it's
time for major *perspiration*.

7

Checklists to Improve Your Poetry

> Poems that lack ideas merely state the obvious—they bore us. Ones that contain ideas, however, unify our thoughts or feelings. They shape how we perceive the world and excite us with images of beauty or moments of truth. —Michael Bugeja

*T*hey say, "You can lead a horse to water, but you can't make him drink." If the horse is hot and thirsty, and the water is pure and cool—no problem. The horse will drink.

Likewise, you can send your poem to an editor, but you can't make him accept it. (When I refer to an editor as "he," of course I include both men and women in that position.) However, if you have done quality work on your poem with your best craft, carefully researched the markets and complied with guidelines, you might find the editor thirsty enough to take a serious look at your submission. Because of the competition, your work needs to stand apart from the crowd by its excellence.

Take the checklists below seriously. They are not exhaustive, but each point may increase the chance that an editor will accept your poem. The checklists pertain primarily to free verse, although they are transferable to traditional rhymed and metered poems. Rewrite, rewrite and rewrite some more. Be ruthless with your blue editing pencil.

Be careful to *avoid* the following:

1. Religious jargon, cliches and expressions understood only by an *in group*. When you deliberately write poems for such a group, that is an exception. Many theological terms come across as "gobbledegook" even to some modern day Christians.

2. Trivial subjects not worth the time to write about, read or market. However, when you write light verse or quatrains for the secular market, that is an exception. Trite, sentimental poems about worn-out subjects without a fresh approach bore the reader. Hackneyed ideas won't cut it. Don't "dash off a poem" and consider it finished. As Patti Garr observed, "True poetry is as planned and carefully assembled as the inspiration behind it."

Paul Bechtel advised his poetry classes:

Remember that you are living in the twentieth century. The world is grappling with issues more urgent than moonlight and roses, lovely as these are. Consider topics like war and peace, science, space exploration, freedom and tyranny, moral issues, the reality of God in a nuclear age and like concerns. Even in these desperate times, perhaps your verse can bring healing to Everyman and his posterity.

However, don't belittle the little themes: ordinary observations you make with your five senses during a stroll, snatches of conversation you hear, homey topics, commonplace things you recall. You can develop these into poems with your fresh perspective and figurative images.

3. Obsolete words such as tis, twas, o'er, ere, 'neath, perchance, thee, thine and wouldst. Shakespeare isn't around anymore, and readers who appreciate such antiquities are becoming fewer. The same applies to word order inversions: said he, I do see, the soldier brave. (See *poetic license* below.)

4. Violation of the rules of good rhyme and meter, if you choose to write in traditional style. This includes stereotyped phrases and overused, obvious rhymes like moon-June, dove-love, trees-breeze, etc.

5. Omission of letters such as mem'ry, hist'ry for the sake of fitting the meter.

6. Obscurity. It is sometimes difficult to understand what so-called "literary" poems are trying to say. Some poets seem to make simple ideas complex, vague and confusing. Present your poem so the reader can, with some serious thought, understand and appreciate it. Deliberate ambiguity to impress is a fad whose time is up. As Janet Chester Bly said, "Clarity wins over obscurity, but the right touch of subtleness charms an editor and a reader."

7. Artificially chopping up narrative lines for the sake of looking like poetry. Some writing would be better as prose.

8. Lack of imagination, imagery, similes, metaphors, personification, etc. Employ nuances of meaning and secondary intimations. We would do well to think about Carl Sandburg's observation, "Poetry is a phantom script telling how rainbows are made and why they go away." We should do more than put random words on paper and call them poetry.

9. Sermons trying to pass as poems. Work on being indirect. Elizabeth Drew advised, "The best religious poetry never preaches; it communicates what it *feels* like to have the poet's faith."

10. Ho-hum dullness. No emotional impact, intellectual stimulation or surprise. The reader loses interest before he finishes the poem because you haven't challenged his emotions or mind. Elva McAllaster advised, "Write poetry from the growing edges of your own present experience, from your present selfhood. That will include the wealth of new reflections and new combinations of former experiences."

11. Mistakes in spelling and violations of grammar. No excuse! That's what spell-check is for on your word processor or why you have a dictionary and Strunk's *The Elements of Style* on your shelf.

12. Common poetry punctuation hangups. Examples are: too many semicolons, overdone dashes and excess exclamation points. Either you've expressed the emotion or you haven't. Punctuation won't create it. Don't overdo ellipses ... to show you are in a dreamy

mood or trailing off your thought. Editors consider such writing amateurish. Punctuation should help the reader, not put obstacles in his way or confuse him.

Be consistent in your punctuation. Opinions differ whether to capitalize the first word of every line, a common practice in English poetry before the turn of the century. Contemporary poets tend not to do so. Use of punctuation continues to be an individual matter.

13. Copying classical styles too closely. Write for today's readers—other readers have passed from the scene. Shun stilted, affected words artificially selected from your thesaurus.

Clement Wood advised, "The vocabulary used by a poet should be the vocabulary he uses in his living speech. Poetry that speaks a dead language is dead from its birth. When real poetry from real poets is encountered, its speech is direct, forthright and living."

What about poetic license?

Poetic license is, of course, not a certificate entitling you to write poetry! The term refers to the privilege claimed by a writer in any genre to deviate from conventional form, established rules, perhaps even fact and logic, to achieve a desired effect.

According to the *Writer's Encyclopedia:*

Writers, particularly poets, have claimed the 'license' when they invert word order, introduce archaisms, use—or overuse—figurative language, employ contractions such as *ere* and *o'er*, and otherwise depart from standards of ordinary speech. But such breaches of grammar, misuse of idiom, mispronunciations for the sake of rhyme, or similar devices are no longer excused in serious verse.

A final questionnaire

1. Do my ideas echo and resound throughout my poem? Is there a recognizable pattern either in lines, stanzas or word repetition?

2. Are the last few lines important or a letdown? Do they sum up, connect, make a dramatic statement or surprise the reader? Have I saved my strongest point for the last? Is it a "clincher?"

3. Have I rambled? Do I need to condense, distill or compress my thoughts and words for maximum impact?

4. Are nouns specific and strong? Is the language concrete?

5. Is the title appropriate, short and appealing? Titles add meaning and grab for the reader's attention. Take them seriously.

Emily Dickinson didn't put titles on any of her poems, but she didn't plan to publish them either. Publishers added titles, usually from her first line, but you should come up with a better idea.

6. Am I accurate in my facts and realistic in my descriptions?

7. Could I omit more adjectives and adverbs? Could I change some into nouns? Or replace most forms of "to be" with sparkling verbs? Are most verbs in the active voice?

8. Have I cut dead words as I would when editing prose? Could I eliminate more connectives and articles?

9. Have I avoided wordiness and expressing the same thing repeatedly without making a fresh point?

10. Have I worked diligently to find the *right* word, the *perfect* phrase—not just one that will do?

11. Have I made full use of the thesaurus, synonym dictionary and rhyming dictionary either in my word processor or from my bookshelf?

12. Have I made the poem sparkle with similes, metaphors, alliteration, allusion, personification and other forms of figurative expression?

13. Is the main theme clear to me and to the reader? Have I focused on only one idea? Does the poem have unity and logical progression?

14. Have I tried to show as well as tell?

15. Have I read my poem *aloud*? Have I ruthlessly critiqued sound, rhythm, language, symbolism and the shape of the poem on paper? Have I read it to anyone and asked if figurative references are clear?

Finally, and foundational, have I asked God to guide me in my thought processes and anoint my meditation so that "the words of my mouth and the meditation of my heart [and my writing] might be acceptable" in God's sight? (Psalm 19:14)

Helps to improve your poetry craft

As Christian poets, we should diligently study our craft as an art form. The following books are among many excellent ones to provide information and inspiration for the writing process of poetry. You ought to study one or more of them carefully. A glance at the Bibliography and Resources pages in the back of this book will suggest others.

The Poet's Handbook by Judson Jerome (Writer's Digest Books) 1507 Dana Avenue, Cincinnati, Ohio 45207 is packed with seasoned instruction on how to use figurative language, symbols and concrete images. He shows us how to tune our ears to sound relationships and how to write different forms of poetry.

Creating Poetry by John Drury (Writer's Digest Books) helps the poet explore and practice poetry writing skills and provides hands-on exercises.

The Art and Craft of Poetry by Michael J. Bugeja, also from Writer's Digest Books, offers helpful, comprehensive information on how to develop yourself as a poet from ideas to creating publishable verse.

The Poet's Guide: How to Publish and Perform Your Work by Michael J. Bugeja, (Story Line Press) Three Oaks Farm, Brownsville, OR 97327 demystifies the business of poetry and provides encouragement for writers to hone their craft. It includes exercises for beginning, intermediate, and advanced poets.

The Poetry Dictionary by John Drury, from Writer's

Digest Books. This comprehensive guide to the poetry of today and yesterday is filled with intriguing hints about what tomorrow holds for the poet.

As you give careful attention to these checklists, an editor may sit up and take notice when you submit a quality poem to him.📖

*S*training too hard to market a poem can dull or kill pure, natural writing. The proper sequence for a poet is to capture ideas and visions on paper, allow the expression to "season," rewrite or set aside again, and *then* begin the marketing process. —Janet Chester Bly

8

To Market—To Market

Poet Luci Shaw wrote, "If you're a poet, you'll be writing poetry whether there's a market for it or not."

*W*riting poetry involves several steps: (1) Observation or awareness of something inward or something outside oneself, (2) Reflection or response to those stimuli, (3) Articulation or creation with the skills peculiar to poetry. The first two are part of the process of ideation. The third is the exercise of the poet's craft.

A fourth step may or may not take place: (4) The poet shares his work. He communicates his poem in some form to others. He may share it through publication in books or periodicals, through formal or informal poetry readings among friends and family or to a wider circle through letters or some other written form. Sharing a poem, however, does not necessarily mean publication in a periodical. Judson Jerome reminded us:

> [To many] the poem doesn't seem quite real until it has been "accepted" by an editor or until it appears in a periodical or a book. It is as though the creative act were dependent for its completion not only upon the judgment of others but upon the vicissitudes of the marketplace. *That isn't true.* A poem exists as soon as it has been composed in the mind. It is "published" as soon as it is written down or recited.

Marketing is the step which bogs down for many excellent poets, aptly expressed by Nellie Jones in *Writers' Journal*, Vol. 16, No. 1, 1995.

Life Cycle of a Poem

There comes a thought all unsought
from somewhere deep inside;
so I grab my pen and rush right in
with a poet's easy stride;
Now I sweat and strain and bruise my brain
all the way to the final draft;
then I stash it away for a year and a day,
my secret, anonymous craft;
And the years slip by as the stack grows high,
for I am still on a roll,
but I cannot bear to have men stare
upon my naked soul.

You may have released the poet within you by writing a poem, but you have clipped its wings because of your shyness or false modesty.

You released your poem from your heart. Now take it out of the drawer, open the window and let it fly out to touch others. (Symbolically!) Your poetry stashed in the drawer of your desk will not give your friends or a wider audience a chance to appreciate it, nor will it accomplish God's plan if you have ministry in mind. There is a time to write and a time to share your work. But remember, *publication does not validate your poetic gift.*

Motives for sharing poetry

I discussed reasons for *writing* poems in chapter one. Some of the motives for a poet to *share his work* are (1) to be appreciated, (2) to influence others, and (3) to make a statement. Influencing others is part of the ministry aspect of writing poetry.

Writing poetry is a lonely art form. Many poets don't know other poets unless they attend conferences or workshops. Every poet wants someone to appreciate his work, as much as a musician is pleased to hear his music performed, or as an artist is gratified when people admire his painting. Like the proud parent of a toddler who is just beginning to babble, the poet tentatively displays his created poem to someone else: "Look at my child. Don't you think she is clever? Do you understand what she is saying?"

It may be reward enough for a poet when someone sees or hears his poem. Payment for writing doesn't matter. Few, if any, poets write for the petty payment an editor might send them. That is why I encourage poets to send their work even to nonpaying markets or those paying in subscriptions to the magazine. That doesn't mean poetry is *cheap*. On the contrary, it may be *priceless!* Judson Jerome summed up what he learned about poetry during his lifetime:

> I have learned a lot. Publication and "success" are not nearly as important as I once thought they were.... If one is serious about poetry, he had better be clear about separating it in his mind from fame and fortune (and advancement). I have learned to respect the promptings, however unskilled their expression, of people who use poetic form to reach out to others. Whether their poems will become immortal contributions to our literature is entirely another question—and not of much immediate concern.

Start with a cold shower!

As far as marketing goes, poetry has a number of strikes against it. Let's get the cold shower out of the way first, and then realistically see how we can warm up to the marketing process. The following are some poetry marketing negatives.

◆ In Bill Moyers' PBS series and book of the same title, *The Language of Life,* he points out, "The market for poetry on the page remains dismal, and many trade publishers have abandoned it. (This has led to a surreal situation in which talented poets sometimes find themselves wishing for rejection; they can't even manage that when publishers refuse to consider their manuscripts.)"

◆ Like any other "fine art," poetry demands professional devotion and ability, yet offers almost none of the rewards that accrue in the non-artistic professions. Most poets also write prose which provides them with more substantial income. We need to be realistic and understand what the rewards of a poet will *not* be. He won't earn a living by it. Poetry, unfortunately, is not a saleable commodity in the same way as a magazine feature, newspaper article, story or novel.

◆ Luci Shaw observed, "Poetry used to be considered the queen of the arts. Now most book publishers don't try to market poetry."

◆ Editors don't want to see poetry submissions on their desks unless they have specifically stated in their publication guidelines that they want them. Even periodicals which accept some poetry can't afford the space to publish many poems per issue.

◆ Let's face it—the public simply isn't interested in poetry. In America comparatively few people read serious books, still fewer read quality literature. Fewest of all read poetry.

◆ Sadly, poetry in magazines is often demeaned to the level of a filler, used only to take up space at the end of articles or stories.

◆ Poetry can't be edited by the editor of a publication like other forms of writing submitted. The editor must take it "as is" or leave it. If it doesn't suit him, he leaves it.

◆ Published collections of poetry receive few, if any, reviews and receive little publicity, therefore poets get little recognition. Grants and awards don't amount to much.

◆ Literary agents don't handle poetry unless the poet also writes other types of literature or is a consistently selling or well-known writer.

◆ Publication of a collection of your poetry in book form almost always requires a fairly established reputation, consistent or broad sales of individual poems to magazines or other periodicals, a substantial number of friends who will buy your books and a considerable outlay of personal funds.

◆ The editor of *Poetry* magazine dumped a whole bucket of cold water on poets who may want to submit poems to that publication:

> If your motives are mercenary, don't bother submitting to our publication. And if they are those of an innocent amateur, don't bother. Nor should you try us if the writing of poetry doesn't seem to you a serious occupation either at the center of your life or very near it. I'd say that anyone who regards the writing of poetry as his hobby, and uses that word for it, shouldn't send us poems, though he might very well sell some of his work elsewhere.

The above is some bad news about trying to market poetry. Don't be discouraged—there is plenty of good news.

The bright side

I briefly referred to the optimistic development regarding poetry in America in my *Preface*. In reviewing television commentator Bill Moyers' book, referred to above, Nicholas Basbanes commented in *The Knoxville News-Sentinel:*

> For those who haven't been paying close attention, it might come as something of a revelation that poetry has been making quite a comeback throughout the United States in recent years. Especially gratifying is that a good deal of excitement for this most elemental of literary forms is being generated by living poets, not just the revered versifiers of the past, a hopeful sign that the creative torch is being passed along from this generation to the next.

Is *my* poetry meant for publication?

We need to be realistic about our poetry gift. Leslie H. Stobbe, Managing Editor of the Curriculum Division of Scripture Press, cautioned in a writers' conference that many Christian poets may not necessarily have been given their gift of poetry *to be published in books or magazines.* He suggested that only a select few may be chosen by God to communicate to that wider audience. Other worthy poets may share their poetry on special occasions in the local church, perhaps for a women's group or at a banquet. Their contribution is important, will be appreciated and can touch lives.

The fact that friends or relatives applaud you, Stobbe said, and think you are a wonderful poet does not necessarily mean you have been called by the Lord to have your poetry *published.* Nor is an inner compulsion to see your poetry in print necessarily evidence of God's call to publication.

Each of us needs to ask the Lord what He has in mind for our expressions in poetry, and accept His direction whether to try for publication—or not.

Why take my poems to the market?

Let's admit it: beyond the satisfaction of expressing ourselves in the poetic mode, poets naturally seek an audience. The poet, holding his precious creation in his hand, or hugging it sentimentally, ventures forth looking for someone to "stop—look—and listen." He needs to share his current masterpiece. Walt Whitman said, "To have great poetry there must be great audiences, too." Most of the poets I know are not necessarily looking for *great* audiences, but for *any* listening ears or seeing eyes. Basically, marketing is searching for an audience for your poetry.

If you do want to try for publication, your best chance for acceptance is to become familiar with the target magazine. Moreover, an editor is more likely to accept shorter poems under twenty lines with the content focused on contemporary, religious and social concerns. Unrhymed poetry is generally more popular. Traditional, rhymed poetry is less preferred for publication today than free verse.

First, consult the writers' market guidebooks. Use a highlighter to mark the periodicals, small magazines, big ones, paying ones, nonpaying ones, every possible category for *your kind of poetry.* A brief paragraph in the guidebooks spells out for you whether a periodical takes poetry and tells you exactly what kind. Look over magazines to which your family and friends subscribe.

Are you a member of a church, denomination or Christian organization? It may publish specialized periodicals whose readers would be interested in your poetry, and through them you could reach your intended audience.

Restrict your submissions to *exactly* what the editor says he wants. Don't try to change his mind by offering him something you think he *ought* to like better.

Don't waste your time, effort and money on futile submissions. If you send poems out blindly without careful targeting, you are only supporting the post office in these days of high postage rates. The rejection slips you will inevitably receive because of ill-advised submissions don't help your self-confidence.

The *listener* market

In past generations, children were told that they should be seen and not heard. On the other hand, poems, your "children" in a sense, are meant to be *both seen and heard.* The poem, like a piece of music, doesn't reach its full potential until it is *heard,* at least in the imagination. The metrical foot of poetry functions like the bar in a musical composition. A trained musician can sit quietly "reading" a piece of music on paper, and, in some sense, he is actually "hearing" it. Judson Jerome commented that "The poem, like a piece of music, doesn't actually exist until it is *heard,* at least in the imagination."

Poet Maya Angelou wrote:

Poetry is music written for the human voice, and what you discover is that it's also written for the human ear. Sound has a meaning apart from the words themselves. The coupling of language and music creates a new experience, an epiphany, in the listener.

The reader usually meets your poem first on the printed page. He must likewise hear it in his imagination, but that is second best. Since you use rhythm, cadence, beat, sometimes rhyme, alliteration and convey emotion, the best exposure for your poem is to have it *heard.*

To listen to a poem from the author's own lips, with his or her distinctive interpretation and inflection, is a treat for audiences.

Ron Mann observed, "When you read a poem, you can sit back and think about it; when you hear it performed by its creator, a new level of passion and personality emerges." These days one doesn't even have to see and hear a poet perform his work in person. CD-ROMS are available for computers and show poets on the display screen reading and discussing their work side by side with easy-to-read texts of their poems.

A poetry reading is one way to go. Readings are excellent performance opportunities to test your work and observe response. Unless you write poetry only for yourself, you should value a relationship with the listener. Art is meant to be appreciated, and writing poetry is both an art and a craft. Readings can take place in libraries, at poetry and literary society meetings, living rooms of homes and in groups meeting anywhere. Don't be shy about making your books available for sale on such occasions.

Readings for children in libraries, if that is your poetry genre, are a fine listening market you should not overlook. You'll soon know whether you have succeeded in writing on a child's level and holding his attention, whether he is bored or excited. Children do not politely hide their feelings. Try the *Poets-in-the-Schools* program, where poets are invited to read their work and interact with children in the classroom.

In the secular field, poetry "slams" in some of the larger cities or college towns have become popular in recent years. They are public poetry competitions in cafes, bars, coffee houses or lounges where poets simply show up and read their work, and members of the audience judge them. Sometimes small monetary prizes are awarded. Someone has described a slam as "a literary version of *The Gong Show*." The poet at the mike might be cheered or booed. Unfortunately, that often makes dramatic presentation more important than quality of craft. The shy poet with less than adequate self-esteem could be devastated by rejection. The flamboyant poet who reads mediocre work could be applauded.

I don't think we have seen the Christian equivalent of slams, nor may we want to—but never say *never*. It may be possible to adapt the concept more positively and sensitively to pre-evangelistic witness.

Publishing on tape

You can actually "publish" your poetry on cassette tapes which you can market as you would books. If you have a collection of your poems, to read it on tape expands your market considerably.

If you want to do the audio production yourself,

record a "master" tape using a high quality microphone (not a mike that is part of the unit) and a recorder with a pause control. You will need to stop and restart the tape between your poems without causing noise that could be heard on tape.

You can make copies of the tapes with a quality dual-cassette player-recorder designed for copying tapes one-to-one. Hand print the title on labels or purchase sheets of labels on which you can type, computer print or photocopy the title and other information.

If you don't have the equipment or confidence to do the above yourself, enlist the help of someone experienced or a professional to achieve high quality recordings. You want to present your best work in the best way.

Give your poems international wings

Don't overlook markets for your poems outside the United States. The editors of Canadian publications and those in the United Kingdom and other English-speaking countries usually have fewer submissions to consider. An international market may await you, especially for reprints or second rights. Consult your local library for market guides listing overseas publications. If you plan to submit poems abroad, buy *International Reply Coupons* (IRCs) at the post office. Those take the place of a foreign country's stamps for editors to use when returning submissions from another country.

The "lighten up!" market

There are specific markets for different kinds of poetry. One example is humor and light verse intended to entertain, amuse or please readers. Certain popular, large circulation general magazines favor humorous verse. Christians may certainly write humor if they use discretion and skill. Both secular and religious markets welcome this lighter touch. Writing it can be fun.

Brevity, seldom more than ten lines, characterizes saleable light verse. The most popular format is the four-liner known as the quatrain. The following example by Rosemarie Williamson, published in the *Good Housekeeping* magazine, was quoted in *Writers' Journal*, Vol. 16, No. 1.

Heavenly Days!

The weather has been brought to you
(This strikes me very odd)
By such and such a sponsorship—
I thought it came from God.

Use conventional rhyme and meter in light verse, keeping it regular and pleasing to the eye as well as the ear. Attract the reader with a snappy title. Anecdotes, one-liners and limericks have a good chance of acceptance. Wit and subtlety rather than depth of literary significance entice an editor. Satire, a twist, the turn of a word, or a common expression are features of this style. Ordinary experiences with which most readers can identify are most popular. Universal themes like dieting, home routines, children, pets, sports—virtually anything can be the subject. Only your imagination and resourcefulness limit you.

Markets for light verse include *Good Housekeeping, McCalls, Saturday Evening Post, Reader's Digest* and greeting card companies.

Helping your poems get to market

A number of publications are available listing specific poetry markets. Be sure to look at *current* editions. Magazines and periodicals often cease publication without notice. Look for markets which solicit the kind of poetry you write.

The *Writer's Market,* published annually by *Writer's Digest Books,* P.O. Box 12948, Cincinnati, Ohio 45212-0948 has copious listings of periodicals that accept poetry. They also publish an annual *Poet's Market* that lists more than 1,700 publishers, conferences, workshops, organizations and poetry contests with much helpful advice on getting your poems published.

The *Poet's Marketplace* by Joseph J. Kelly, Running Press, 129 South 22nd St. Phila. PA 19103 is another definitive source book on where to get your poems published.

An excellent *Poet's Handbook* compiled by Lincoln B. Young is published by Fine Arts Press, P.O. Box 3491, Knoxville, Tennessee 37927 with over 2,300 poetry publishers listed.

In secular market guides you will find listings for publications such as Literary Quarterlies, Literary Journals, Poetry Journals, Literary Digests and Reviews, University Quarterlies, "Little" magazines, monthlies, newspapers, trade journals and organizational or house organs which accept poetry. Consult your local library for addresses.

Marketing Christian poetry

In the category of Christian poetry, each annual edition of *The Christian Writers' Market Guide* by Sally E. Stuart, Harold Shaw Publishers, Box 567, Wheaton, IL 60189 publishes many pages listing magazines which accept poetry and tells you exactly what kind they look for.

The Guide to Religious and Inspirational Magazines compiled by Elizabeth Gould and Livia Fiordelisi, Writer's Resources, 53 Brandon Road, Milton, MA 02186, profiles over 500 publications listing poetry markets among other writings solicited.

Don't overlook an important ministry market for your poetry—your friends. Write "word gifts" and "one-time specials" for a friend facing surgery, a parent confronting an empty nest, a neighbor coping with grief or a retiree adjusting to his new schedule. One Christian friend is constantly asked to write personalized poems for weddings which she frames as gifts. Friends and relatives will cherish personal birthday poems.

I wrote a personalized poem celebrating the birth

of my seventh grandchild. I made a computer printout in a
script font, photo-copied it on parchment paper and
framed it as a gift for my son and daughter-in-law.

My Granddaughter, Brianna Arlene Choy
Born March 6, 1995

Rejoice, rejoice, all our ancestors!
Throw a party on the golden streets
of eternity! Cheer ecstatically—
Brianna has been born
to our family tree . . .
a generational progeny!

God formed her from our *DNA*
bequeathed from ages past.
When she's grown,
this bundle of potentiality,
God will pass on through her
our inherited legacy
to her posterity.

Hear my prayer, O Lord!
I present this child to You,
whom You predestined
for her place in history,
whom You chose
from the foundation of the world.
What an awesome mystery
that You've determined
Brianna's destiny!
May her first cry be

praise-music to Your ears
thanking You
for Your breath of life.

Grant Theresa and Gary joy
and wisdom for their holy task
of guiding Brianna,
child of the covenant,
on the path of earthly life
and Life Eternal.
May she know You
as her Heavenly Father
and take her appointed place
with saints of all ages
singing praises in Your presence
with all her genetic forebears
from Ireland and China,
Germany, England,
Czechoslovakia and America!

Church bulletins and monthly newsletters could be appreciative markets for your poems. People sometimes send church mailings to shut-ins and friends at large, and your poems might reach an even wider readership. Even poetry which professional critics might judge to be less than artistically excellent may serve important functions for its author and bring pleasure and enrichment to other people.

Opportunities abound to write poems for special events. The custom of appointing a *poet laureate* began in Great Britain where the royal household commissioned a person to write poems to celebrate court and national events. Ben Jonson was the first appointee in 1619. In the United States some states choose their own poets laureate. They don't need to be well-known, are usually appointed for life, and more than one person may hold the position simultaneously.

Perhaps you can be God's appointed poet laureate to write poems celebrating people and events in your church, your family and your world.

Your reward will come from the satisfaction that God used your words to encourage others. You might write a *poem with a purpose* for a specific friend and have the joy of knowing that it accomplished its purpose as a valued personal gift with a message. It's not likely your friend would send you a rejection slip! However, the Lord might have a plan to extend the poem's influence beyond that "one-time special." Sometimes my friends tell me they receive new insights from a poem in which I express my life experience. They ask permission to copy and send it to *their* friends, passing its influence on and on.

I have a long time friend, Evelyn, who is the editor of an international Christian magazine of wide circulation. Her minister husband died suddenly, and I sent her one of my poems intended for her personal comfort. She asked permission to publish it and wanted to see more poems. My poetry appeared almost monthly for about five years on the back cover of her magazine with full color art work. The magazine pays me $20 a poem—that's a bonus dinner in a restaurant with a friend once a month.

Most of us have seen poems published in books on every subject from Bible studies to recipe books. Other ministry possibilities for your inspirational poems are plaques, needlework, posters, banners, quilts, kitchen magnets, bookmarks and calendars. Look through a novelty gift catalog and see how many potential formats your poetry could have. Consider framing your favorite poems as Christmas or special occasion gifts.

Greeting card verse

Greeting cards is another ministry avenue for your poetry. You can produce your own cards economically and bring delight to people in your world. Using your original poetry in them is distinctive.

Keep your poems short and uniquely targeted for the occasion. Try non-occasion cards expressing messages not tied to certain dates. That's where your creativity comes in. Simple art work or your own sketches or line drawings can enhance your poetry.

If you create greeting cards strictly for your world and don't sell them or make a business of it, you don't need to worry about copyright. If you reach the point where you produce cards for wider use and sell them for others to send, you should consult Sally Stuart's book *Copyright Not Copycat: A Writer's Guide to Copyright*, available from *The Christian Communicator*. Larry Sandman's book, *A

Guide to Greeting Card Writing (Writer's Digest Books, 1980) is also useful. The *Greeting Card Writer's Handbook* edited by H. Joseph Chadwick (Writer's Digest Books) has practical information on every phase of getting ideas, writing and selling greeting cards.

How *to Write and Sell Greeting Cards, Bumper Stickers, T-shirts and Other Fun Stuff* by Molly Wigand (Writer's Digest Books). The author is a veteran of Hallmark card writing. Her comprehensive book covers the ins and outs of writing in a media ripe for your message. Although written for the secular market, this book has a section devoted to "Inspirational and Religious" cards.

Consult the current edition of *The Christian Writers' Market Guide* by Sally E. Stuart for a special section on greeting card markets.

If your cards are especially well-received, you might approach your local Christian bookstore about taking some on consignment.

Formula for (some) success

The following formula usually gives you a good shot at successful marketing: Quality work + careful market study + the right format + complying with the publication's guidelines + the right timing = acceptance. Hopefully, *some* of the time!

You've followed the above formula and editors still reject your poetry? Don't view an editor as your opponent or enemy. He or she is really on your side, often called to edit as much as you are called to write. Trust

God through the editor. Keep writing, revising, improving and submitting your work to different markets.

Viola Jacobson Berg advised, "Let us learn to take rejections gracefully without losing heart. Each aspiring poet has to come to the place in his own life when he accepts rejection as a part of learning. If this doesn't happen, he will never go far."■

*E*ditors expect professionalism.
When you comply with the
simple, broadly-accepted rules of
manuscript submission, you
earn their respect.

9

Mechanics of Submitting Poetry

Check your market guidebooks to be sure you conform to a particular editor's requirements. Keep accurate records of what you send, when you send it and the response.

*S*hould you enclose a cover letter when submitting poetry to an editor? Some practices are changing. I understood we should not do so. Increasingly, however, editors request such letters. Likewise, the jury is still out on whether it's advisable to tell an editor how much you like his magazine. That used to be another no-no, not only unnecessary but unprofessional. Now they tell us that some editors appreciate a little genuine affirmation of their job well done. We should, of course, give sincere compliments not flattery. Such comments turn off other editors, we understand. Check your market guidebooks so you will know what an editor expects.

Your cover letter should not try to "explain" your poem, how it "came to you" or declare that "words just flowed as if God dictated them." The letter may include businesslike information about yourself, publishing credits and the titles of poems you enclosed. A cover letter may give you a chance to develop a connection with an editor. If you have no publishing credits, don't be tempted to say you've been writing poems since second grade. In that case, it might be better to omit the cover letter. Keep it to no more than 100 or 200 words. Edit and tighten your words as you would a piece of prose.

Never include a photo of yourself, illustrations, etc. To be professional use plain paper generally without personalized letterhead that shows your title as "poet," a dead giveaway that you are an amateur probably submitting a substandard manuscript. Be sure to let the editor know if the poems you enclose were previously published or if they are simultaneous submissions.

Use 8-1/2 x 11 inch white paper and submit originals or high quality photocopies. Be sure to keep file copies. If you type, use fresh ribbons. If you use a word processor, don't use fancy fonts to appear poetic. You shouldn't send handwritten poems. If you don't type, find someone to type for you. Neatness is important. If you submit a reprint, don't send a photocopied tear sheet of your poem that another magazine published. Type it over on a fresh sheet.

Type your name, address and telephone number in the upper right corner along with your social security number. Type the publishing rights you offer in the upper left. You don't need to state the number of words or lines in your poem. Periodicals, if they pay, usually pay a flat fee, not according to the number of words as they do for prose. If you wish to state copyright, put the copyright symbol, © followed by the word *copyright*, the current year and your name—all at the top right.

Type the title of your poem flush left or centered, using all capital letters or initial caps. Drop down two lines and type your poem single spaced, one poem on a page and double spaced between stanzas. Type your name once more a few lines below the end of the poem.

If your poem is longer than one page, type your name (address is optional) at the top left margin of each additional page. Underneath, in parentheses, a key word from the title or the whole title if it is short, with the page number and stanza information.

Below is how it might appear on a second page:

Leona Choy
("A Time to Pick," page 2, begin new
stanza) or (continue stanza)

Drop down about six spaces and continue typing the poem on the second page. Never type on the reverse side of the paper. Don't use staples or paper clips. Proof-read your poem again after typing. Nothing turns off an editor more than misspellings, typos and grammatical and punctuation errors.

Keep accurate records of which poems you have submitted and where you have sent them. Record the date and the result on index cards or in file folders along with the original of the poem.

Never send any submission to an editor or publisher without enclosing a self-addressed, stamped envelope (SASE). No exceptions. Otherwise, the editor might trash your submission. If you want him to return your poems, be sure the SASE is large enough to hold all the poems without refolding them. You must put on enough postage—the same amount you put on the outside mailing envelope.

Typically, three pages plus a cover letter and SASE (four pages total) take one first class stamp on a #10 legal size envelope. Weight of paper varies, so weigh some sample submissions to be sure. If an editor receives your submission *postage due,* he may do more than growl. He may refuse it.

Place all sheets neatly together, then fold the entire group into thirds as if it were one sheet. The return envelope should be the same size and folded into thirds. Don't use cardboard backing. If you send less than six pages, use a #10 outer envelope. If seven to ten pages, use a 6 x 9 envelope. If more than ten, a 9 x 12 envelope.

You may want to arrange your poems in some tantalizing sequence that might attract an editor to continue reading. Perhaps your best poem first—or last, if you want to leave a final impression. Send either a variety of poems or a collection on one theme. Your choice will depend on the guidelines of the publication, your own stock of poems and style of writing.

If you don't want the editor to return your poems, (to save return postage and because you send disposable copies) state your instructions briefly in your cover letter.

Nevertheless, enclose a #10 SASE with first class postage for the answer.

There is seldom any reason to use a pen name. If the editor wants to send you a check, different names confuse him. Be consistent in the use of your name as author. Not Mrs. Woodbe Wrighter on one poem, Hope Wrighter or I.M.A. Wrighter on another poem.

Copyright or not?

According to the current *Poet's Market,* (Writer's Digest Books) "Copyright notices on poems, even on book-length manuscripts, are usually unnecessary. Some editors believe that those who use the symbol are amateurs overly concerned about literary theft."

Should you copyright your poem as soon as you write one? According to the copyright law effective January 1, 1978, the creator of any piece of writing has all rights as soon as the particular work is complete. He may sell all or part of those rights. That means your work is copyrighted by common law until you publish it. Most editors take for granted that you own the copyright, but they usually won't mind if you use the copyright symbol.

When you wish to show copyright, follow the procedure previously given. You don't need to register any piece of writing directly with the Copyright Office.

No one may republish your copyrighted work without your permission, and you may request a fee from them for the privilege, if you wish.

Most magazines are copyrighted.
However, if you do not indicate copyright
on your poem and a periodical that is not
copyrighted publishes it, it becomes
"public domain."

Public domain means that anyone can use it without paying a fee. When a person or another periodical writes to the magazine which published your poem to ask for permission to reprint your poem, the editor customarily forwards the request to the author as a matter of courtesy.

Many literary magazines and other publications which accept freelance submissions, especially poetry, are not copyrighted. Anyone who wishes may use your writing or reprint your poem without notifying you. He may even put his or her own name on your poem. That may be reason enough for you to go ahead and be safe by using the copyright symbol on all your writing.

What rights to offer

Unless you tell them otherwise, editors assume that your submitted work is original, not previously published elsewhere, and not submitted to another magazine. If you send the same poems elsewhere at the same time, you are offering *simultaneous rights*. You may want to do that because some magazines are incredibly slow to respond, taking as long as a year to reject or accept a poem. You may send poems to two or more publications (whose circulations do not overlap) at the same time, but you *must* let both editors know. Some editors will take a look at simultaneous submissions, some won't. Some actually consider it an insult to be offered a reprint. By all means, consult your market guide.

If you do go the simultaneous submission route, and one editor accepts one or more of your poems, phone or write *each* of the other editors immediately to withdraw *all* your poems, not just the one accepted elsewhere. If the editor asks for an explanation, simply tell the truth. If, on the slim chance that two publications accept the same poem at the same time, you should write a letter of apology to the publication you want to decline. If that upsets the editor, perhaps you shouldn't submit poems to that market again—your chances of acceptance would probably be nil.

Most market guidebooks state the expected response time for a submission. Don't hold your breath for a reply, however. Move on to write other things. If you haven't heard for perhaps twice the stated period, you may write a polite letter to ask the status of your submission or when the editor expects to make a decision. Don't phone and don't pressure an editor. Enclose a return postcard or another SASE. If he doesn't reply after about a month or two, inform the publication by postcard of the date of your original submission, the date of your inquiry, and *politely* withdraw all your poems. List them by title. Never respond with anger or complaint. Those are signs of an amateur.

When you offer *first rights or first serial rights* to a periodical, the editor takes for granted that his periodical will be the first to publish the material. You can modify this by restricting it to first North American serial rights or first U.S. serial rights. The word *serial* has nothing to do with a series. It is simply another word for periodicals. When you offer first rights, copyright reverts to you after publication.

When an editor buys *all rights* to a piece, the writer permanently loses all rights to offer it for sale again to another publisher. You no longer own that poem. Some publications buy only all rights. If you sold all rights and want to use your poem elsewhere later or reprint your poems in a future collection, you must write to the publisher of *each* published poem to request a release.

When you offer *second serial rights,* (reprints) the editor understands that another periodical already published the writing. Consult the market guide for publications willing to consider second rights.

When selling to a market abroad, you offer *foreign serial rights,* provided you still have the rights. For example, if you sold first U.S. serial rights to an American magazine, you are free to market the same piece in Europe. However, if a U.S. editor purchased "first serial rights" without any limiting phrase, he may also be the publisher of foreign editions of his magazine. He correctly assumes that he has the right to be the first to publish your writing in any country in the world.

Dealing with rejection—
and acceptance

Michael Bugeja from his vantage point as a professional poet and professor of journalism advised:

> Prepare to be rejected. I receive six rejections
> for every acceptance. While I publish almost every
> poem I compose, my logs show that sometimes the
> process can take 10 years. One poem written in 1982
> was sent to 42 magazines, accepted in 1990, and
> published in 1992.

When an editor sends you a rejection slip, it is not
the end of the world. There are many reasons why an
editor might reject your poem. Take heart—a rejected
poem doesn't reflect on your worth as a person or on
the literary merit or message of your poem. Some (perhaps tongue-in-cheek!) reasons an editor might reject
your poem:

- The editor didn't sleep well last night
- He missed his breakfast
- Too busy and skipped lunch
- The coffee machine broke down
- He had a headache
- Just got back from vacation, work piled up
- Time pressure toward a deadline
- Had a "bad hair day"
- Weather affected his arthritis
- Argument with a spouse or significant other
- Had poison ivy
- You violated some of my chapter 7 checklists

- Personal prejudices about the topic
- He received too many similar poems
- His poetic style preference
- He spilled coffee on your poems and can't read them
- You didn't follow his published guidelines
- He's limited in space for poetry
- He saw your poem just before quitting time.

Humor aside, an editor who can only publish 100 poems a year, may receive 2,000-3,000 poetry submissions annually. However, an editor is always looking for good submissions because his job depends on the quality of his publication. An editor must stick to the editorial platform of his magazine, and he is obligated to cater to the tastes of his readers or subscribers.

Treat an editor with respect and recognize that he is human. He tries to be fair, but is not always right. Have you thought of praying for him?

An editor may reply with either of two kinds of rejection slips: a standard printed one or a personal note. The second kind is more encouraging, and after some time, you might try to submit other poems to that publication. Sometimes an editor returns your submission without any rejection slip. That might have been an oversight. Don't be offended, just forget it and submit elsewhere.

Sometimes an editor will take time to suggest changes—a new title or minor revision—because he knows what his readers like. An editor cannot make changes in your poem as he might in a feature article you submit to him. A poem is uniquely your creation. If the editor says that he won't accept your poem unless you make the changes, you may either do so or decline to do the revision. It's your call.

If revision will truly improve your poem, be humble about it and consider the suggestion a happy bonus. If you feel the changes would be too drastic, if the editor is injecting his own words or thoughts into your poem, or the changes might weaken or alter your intent, you may politely decline. Try not to be defensive or initiate a lengthy correspondence with the editor. He is too busy for that.

Your poem may be publishable elsewhere as is. I would advise, however, that you take an objective look at your poem and think about editing it again before you submit it elsewhere. You might find that some of the suggested changes would work.

If you make the changes, and the editor accepts your revised poem, you might find an open door for more of your work. A substantial foot in the door is worth some extra work and eating a slice of humble pie.

Consider rejections a part of your education as a poet. Don't feel personally attacked, lose heart or decide to give up.

When an editor sends you a rejection slip, never write back to ask him for a reason. Editors are usually overworked. They can't spend valuable time critiquing an unsolicited piece of writing. Learn from your experience and move on. Keep honing your skills and get ready to send your poem off to another market.

*W*hat do the following poets
and authors have in common?
Walt Whitman, Henry David
Thoreau, Benjamin Franklin,
Thomas Paine, Robert Burns,
Washington Irving, Percy
Shelley, Lord Byron, Edgar Allen
Poe, Mark Twain, Upton Sinclair,
Carl Sandburg, James Joyce,
William Faulkner and Ernest
Hemingway.
They all *self-published* their
works at sometime in their lives!

10

Self-publishing—A Legitimate Option

Michael Bugeja says, "Every poet has an obligation to publish his verse. Other than doing readings, this is the only way for your work to reach an audience."

*A*dmittedly, as Don Marquis reflected, "Publishing a volume of verse is like dropping a rose petal down the Grand Canyon and waiting for the echo." But there comes a time when a poet who has compiled a number of his best poems or a collection on a certain theme wants to publish it in book or chapbook form.

Publishing alternatives for collections of your poetry are several:

(1) *Standard publishing.* Customarily, the publisher of a book pays all production costs and the author receives a small royalty, usually about ten percent, either on the wholesale or retail price. On some arrangements the author receives no royalties but gets ten percent of the

press run.

However, few conventional book publishers even agree to look at a poetry manuscript because a publisher knows from experience that he can't make money on books of poetry. Notable exceptions are books of poetry written by Ruth Graham, Catherine Marshall, Luci Shaw or some other well-known person.

(2) *Cooperative publishing.* This is the share-the-burden route. The author co-finances the project with the publisher. Be sure that you fully understand the terms and can fulfill your part of the financial arrangements. In such an agreement, you pay part of the costs of production, printing and sometimes marketing and promotion.

(3) *Self-publishing,* also known as *independent publishing.* This legitimate option is an increasingly popular and practical route of sharing your poetry with others. Self-publication is an honorable route which any poet today may pursue. At its simplest, if you have access to a photo copy machine and a stapler, you have no reason to go unpublished.

Judson Jerome declared, "If poetry is your *hobby,* you have the right to spend your money to promote it. That is no more vain or indulgent than spending it on golf equipment, woodworking or needlework. You are forthrightly sharing an artistic accomplishment and handing down something of value to your descendants."

Charles A. Waugaman, author of six books of poetry and hundreds of published poems, said, "All my books are self-published. I have a friend who printed most of them. They are handset, hand-assembled and bound, limited editions. I am an artist so I illustrate my own books. . . . This is not just self-flattery."

Why not self-publish?

Self-publishers are in good company. Many famous writers of today and yesterday published their own work at some time during their careers. Walt Whitman printed the first edition of *Leaves of Grass* by setting it up letter-by-letter in the print shop of a friend. He then wrote glowing reviews of his book under several assumed names and sent them to newspapers and magazines! Henry David Thoreau had 1,000 copies of his poetry book printed but sold only 300 copies in his lifetime. All the writers listed on the previous page published some of their own writings—*so why not you?* Laurel Speer advised:

> We all know we write poems because we're compelled by other aspects of our lives that drive us mad from within, but once having served those clamoring voices, publishing the poem is a definite next. Without publication, there is no poem except for the poet and a few patient friends who might consent to listen or read. So it is important we get those words out onto a printed page. Otherwise, we are just talking to the wall.

How does it work?

In a self-publishing arrangement, you, the author, decide on a name for your "press" or publishing entity and pay all actual expenses connected with the book's manufacture: typesetting, printing, cover design, binding and marketing. You own all the books and you keep all income derived from their sale.

Be prepared that family, friends and relatives will exert loving pressure on you to give them complimentary copies. You should ask yourself whether you can realistically expect enough profit from book sales to warrant your investment—if you expect a return. But if you don't care about making a profit, if you are happy to give away copies, (there's nothing wrong with that) you have no problem. You only need enough money for the production.

Face the hard facts—you will, of course, have to market your books. Marketing self-published books is not easy, but can be more successful when you have a specific readership and a cost-effective way to reach them. If you are a speaker or involved in an organization or ministry, you have a built-in market.

You may compile your poems into a book if you have enough poems, or into a booklet or chapbook. Chapbooks are slim poetry volumes of 25 pages or so, usually on a single theme. They typically sell few copies, most are shared with friends as complimentary copies. They largely build confidence for a poet or serve as a ministry. My chapbook of computer poems, *Divine Applications,* falls into that size category.

Self-publishing can be done well or crudely. The Christian writer should not do anything in a slovenly manner. He should seek good advice and help from experienced friends, if he needs it, to produce a high quality product. Public libraries carry helpful books on every aspect of self-publishing and marketing. If you are buying only one book, I would suggest *The Successful Self-Publisher: Produce and Market Your Own Best Seller,* by Dorothy Kavka and Dan Heise, 1996 (Evanston Publishing, Inc.) Evanston, IL 60201. Among others are *The Complete Guide To Self-Publishing* by Tom and Marilyn Ross (Writer's Digest Books) and *The Self-Publishing Manual* by Dan Poynter, (Para Publishing) Santa Barbara, California.

Judson Jerome gave poets a major shove toward trying to self-publish:

> You don't need anyone's permission to be a publisher, i.e., to arrange to have your books printed and then to offer them for sale or distribution. Just do it! Take your life in your hands. Do you want to have readable copies of your work, reasonably attractive, to sell at readings or, at least, to give away? Do yourself a favor and satisfy that urge.

If you decide to take the plunge and self-publish, I advise short press runs of 100 to 500 copies although that makes the cost per copy higher than if you printed a greater quantity. But you probably need to leave some room in your garage to park your car and not fill it with cases of books you can't get rid of. Moreover, if you sell out and need to reprint, the "Second Printing" notation looks good!

But *avoid* subsidy publishing!

Beware of a deceivingly similar but vastly different publishing route. *Subsidy publishers,* or "vanity" publishers, as they are commonly called, actively solicit books by flattering the author. The *Poet's Market* advises, "Avoid these. Nobody respects them. They count on your general ignorance of publishing."

Judson Jerome wrote, "Vanity press is a high-cost printing business which parasitically imitates the conventional publishers."

In subsidy publishing, the author pays the publisher to produce a book for him, an investment with the prospect of little or no return. Not only does the author finance the *entire* production, as in self-publishing, but the subsidy publisher profits on every book he produces. He pads the actual costs to assure himself of a profit on the initial production of the book. Therefore, he may not really care whether or not the book sells.

In the subsidy process, the author does not have control of the whole project as in self-publishing. The author pays out more money to have the book printed by a subsidy publisher than he would if he self-published with an independent printer. In some vanity contracts, the author doesn't even own the books he paid to publish. He receives a few free "author's copies," then is "given the privilege" of buying more copies at the "author's discount."

The review copies which the subsidy publisher promises to send out often go straight into the wastebasket because periodicals or reviewers recognize the name of the subsidy publisher on the spine of the book. They are reluctant to recommend it. Subsidy publishers are known for doing a "snow job" on the author by printing a few "news releases" which may not even be mailed. Bookstores are rarely willing to accept vanity press books to retail.

Generally, subsidy publishers accept any book manuscript whether or not it is saleable, quality writing. They are out to make a profit on the author. Please understand, what subsidy publishers do is *not unethical*. Business is business. *If* the author is aware of all arrangements and understands and agrees with all the small print in the contract, he is certainly free to contract with a vanity publisher. Most professional writers recommend against it, but any author has a right to do as he chooses.

Vanity publishers promote their services widely in writers' magazines. In a current issue of *Writers' Digest*, several such advertisements by subsidy publishers appear: *Vantage Press, Inc., Dorrance Publishing Co., Carlton Press and Rutledge Books.*

What about contests?

Entering poetry contests is often indirectly related to publishing. Surprised? The publishing aspect is often hidden in the advertising, but sooner or later, if you have a winning contest poem, you may encounter some "come-on" of which you should be aware and *beware*. As you flip the pages of magazines like *The Writer* and *Writer's Digest*, you are teased and tempted by contest announcements:

> *"Poetry Contest: Win $1000 cash. $30,000 in prizes and gifts. No entry fee (or a fee, in some cases). Free publication of winners." "Poetry contest, $24,000 awarded annually and possible publication of your poem." "New poets welcome, $15,000 cash and prizes." "Poet of the Year $5,000 prize package contest."*

Enticing! Why not try? Great opportunity to cash in on your work! Some of these are *bona fide* contests, but many are hooks to draw you deeper than you expected. Some of them accept almost any submitted poem and then try to persuade you to buy an expensive volume of the compiled anthology in which your poem will appear. If you are thinking about entering a contest, send for complete details *before* you take the plunge. *Be sure to read all the small print carefully* with a clear head. Be careful of contests requiring you to send entry money for each poem you submit.

Especially beware of responding to advertising like *"Poems Wanted for Songs and Records." "Songs composed from your poems. Cash. Recording opportunities. Publishing awards." "Songwriters! Poets! Spiritual and religious poems and lyrics wanted for musical setting and recording."*

Judson Jerome used strong words to caution us against the above kind of advertising:

"Contests with 'Poems Wanted' should constitute a red flag. No one *wants* poems. What they want is *your money,* and they will ply your vanity to find a way to get it."

Such people are the charlatans of the music business according to Lincoln B. Young, author of *Poet's Handbook.* He goes on to say:

> They are known by the *Better Business Bureau* as "song sharks." Their genius lies not in composing a suitable melody for your "song," but in the clever methods they have devised for raiding the billfolds and bank accounts of unsuspecting amateur poets. They have no connections with the legitimate world of music. Real music publishers and record companies shun them like a fatal epidemic. So should you!

Once upon a time (a true story, believe me) one of my young Christian friends worked in a professional office as secretary. She decided she would like to be a poet. She had never written anything, certainly not a poem. She dashed off two poems, a four-liner and an eight-liner. She saw one of the hook advertisements like the above in a magazine. She sent off the eight-liner titled "Friendship" and received a flattering letter from the publisher praising her outstanding talent.

They "chose" her poem to be set to music. *However,* they enclosed a contract with small print requiring her to pay a substantial sum of money up front for the musical production. She also had to promise in writing to buy a large quantity of record albums on which her song would be *one of many.* And she had to promote the record herself.

Puffed with ego, she stopped her ears to any cautions from experienced writers. She thought of herself as "a discovered poet" and began living on "cloud nine." She printed business cards with "Poet" under her name. You wouldn't believe how much she paid the record company!

Now on a roll and blinded by her "success," she entered another contest with her only other poem, the four-liner about a butterfly. The publisher sent her an Honorable Mention certificate and invited her to Florida for a resort weekend where she would receive her award with other newly discovered poets at a gala banquet. She was responsible for all her expenses, of course, and a fancy, full-color brochure spelled out the high costs.

They convinced her that she was on her way to a poetry career. She went, and for that one weekend she spent about $2,000—all her savings.

Guess what? She isn't writing poetry anymore!

Watch out! Those of us who write poetry have vulnerable egos. We may become victims in the dog-eat-dog publishing world. We are easy targets for those who would take advantage of our hunger for recognition.

Cautions and checkpoints

Some contests are legitimate. However, according to the current *Poet's Market,* we should be aware that contests are often geared not to celebrate poets or their works but to generate start-up funds for new publications, to increase readership or make a profit. Generally, reputable contests require that your submission be un-published and not under consideration elsewhere. Contests sometimes tie up your poems and keep them out of circulation for up to a year, which may make you think twice before entering.

Many magazines charge entry fees to cover costs of judging, handling and prizes. Typical entry fees range between $1-5 per poem. Be suspicious of anything higher. You would do well to request lists of previous winners to be sure it is a legitimate, ongoing contest. Obey all contest rules meticulously. One slip may disqualify your entry, and contest officials might not feel obligated to notify you. You might be waiting hopefully but in vain for the outcome of a contest in which you were no longer in the running.

Ruth Daigon, editor of *Poets On,* cautions us against many "operators" out there. She recommends we watch out for the contest where everyone wins, that it's a marketing device to sell books at inflated prices. Sometimes, she says, sponsors have already made their decisions long before the contest has been announced and are merely raising funds to publish the poets of their choice. This may occur with perfectly respectable organizations. So why does *she* still enter selected contests year after year? She explains:

> Because it's still well worth the effort, not necessarily because you're going to enjoy instant fame but because the greatest reward is the fact that you work and rework your poems in preparation for the event. You push yourself to the limit and spend the necessary time a finished work demands.

Among the reputable contests is the annual one, conducted for decades, by *Writer's Digest* magazine. It is based on merit considerations. The *Poets and Writers* magazine has an 800 number where one can make inquiries about contests advertised in their magazine. Those listed in *Poet's Market* are generally trustworthy.

What would give you a chance to place your poem in one of the legitimate contests? You need to be persistent. Keep entering each year until you win at some level or are satisfied you've tried your best. Read the poems of previous winners. Try to meet some of the winners and get their suggestions. You should send only your best, painstakingly edited work.

And don't hold your breath until that one contest is judged. Keep on writing more poems and submitting them to other publications.

Off the Launching Pad

Are you ready to release the poet within you?

● As a Christian poet, don't let anything dim your determination to please your Supreme Editor, God.

● Do your personal best with the gift the Lord has given you and opportunities He sets before you.

● Work diligently on the craft of poetry so that you may serve the Lord with quality writing enhanced by the anointing and direction of His Spirit.

● Don't compare yourself with other poets or measure yourself against their publishing credits.

Reader applause doesn't validate your identity as a Christian poet. Publication doesn't affect your worth. Nor do you need literary critics or your friends to affirm your work. Make it your heart motive to write "verses for the King" to glorify Him. The Lord will decide whether you will be widely published or never published.

As a Christian poet, you don't win the prize by entering a contest. You "press on toward the goal for the prize of the upward call of God in Christ Jesus" (Philippians 3:14). When you hear His "Well done, good and faithful servant," that will be reward enough, won't it?

This book is intended to be a launching pad.

Did the Lord challenge you to get serious about beginning your poetry writing journey? Or improve the quality of your craft? Or use your gift of poetry for ministry? *Then it is time for action!*

Let's determine, with the Lord's help,
to *release the poet within!*

The End

Bibliography and Resources

Instead of peppering the text with footnotes or references to End Notes, the author has chosen to acknowledge quotations by book and author in the bibliography below.

Acknowledgment of Quotations from Books

The Complete Rhyming Dictionary and Poet's Craft Book, edited by Clement Wood, 1936, Blue Ribbon Books, Doubleday & Co., Inc. Garden City, New York.

Writing Poetry: Where Poems Come From and How to Write Them, David Kirby, 1994, The Writer, Inc. 120 Boylston St., Boston, MA 02115-4615.

How to Read a Poem, Burton Raffel, 1984, A Meridian book published by the Penguin Group, 375 Hudson St., New York, New York, 10014.

On Being a Poet, Judson Jerome, 1984, Writer's Digest Books, 1507 Dana Ave., Cincinnati, Ohio 45207.

Publishing Poetry, Judson Jerome, 1981, Cedar Rock Press, 1121 Madeline, New Braunfels, Texas, 78130.

The Poet and the Poem, Judson Jerome, 1974, Writer's Digest Books, 1507 Dana Ave., Cincinnati, Ohio 45207.

Poet's Handbook, Lincoln B. Young, 1991, Fine Arts Press, P.O. Box 3491, Knoxville, TN 37927.

The Poet's Marketplace, Joseph J. Kelly, Running Press, 125 South 22nd St., Phila., PA 19103.

The Poet's Market, 1996 edition, edited by Michael J. Bugeja and Christine Martin, Writer's Digest Books, 1507 Dana Ave., Cincinnati, Ohio 45207.

The Art and Craft of Poetry, Michael J. Bugeja, 1994, Writer's Digest Books, 1507 Dana Ave., Cincinnati, Ohio 45207.

Poet's Guide: How to Publish and Perform Your Work, 1995, Story Line Press, Three Oaks Farm, Brownsville, OR 97327.

Creating Poetry, John Drury, 1995, Writer's Digest Books, 1507 Dana Ave., Cincinnati, Ohio 45207.

The Poetry Dictionary, John Drury, 1996, Writer's Digest Books, 1507 Dana Ave., Cincinnati, Ohio 45207.

Writer's Encyclopedia, edited by Kirk Polking, 1983, Writer's Digest Books, 1507 Dana Ave., Cincinnati, Ohio 45207.

Christian Writers' Market Guide, 1996, Sally E. Stuart, Harold Shaw Publishers, Box 567, Wheaton, IL 60189.

Acknowledgment of Quotations from Periodicals

Visual and Aural, Judson Jerome, article in *Writer's Digest,* September 1984.

Language of Life, Bill Moyers, 1995, Doubleday, (Book review in *The Knoxville News-Sentinel,* June 25, 1996.)

"I'm Ed, and I'm a Poet," Television review, Brad Leithauser, *Time* magazine, July 3, 1995.

The Choice for Poetry, C.D. Wright, Article in *The Writer,* May 1993.

Poets, Learn Your Trade, Robert Mezey, Article in *The Writer,* February 1993.

Writing Humor and Light Verse That Sells, Rosemarie Williamson, article in *The Writer,* July 1993.

On Writing a Poem, Larry Brook, article in *Interlit* Magazine, March 1989.

Writing Inspirational Poetry, Interview by Patti Garr with contemporary Christian poets, *The Christian Writer,* April 1984.

Monkey, Moon, and Laundry, Larry Brook, article in *Interlit* Magazine, December 1989.

To Climb These Mountains, Elva McAllaster, article in *The Christian Writer,* April 1984.

Who's Afraid of Poetry? Rita Dove, article in Writer's Digest, February 1995.

The Poetic Life of Luci Shaw, Interview by Marian Flandrick Bray, article in *The Christian Communicator,* March 1994.

How to Publish Your Poetry, Ruth E. McDaniel, article in *The Christian Communicator,* October 1994.

Writing Her River, Vicki Huffman, Interview with Luci Shaw, article in *A Better Tomorrow* magazine, March/April 1995.

Crossover Poems, Michael J. Bugeja, Poetry column in *Writer's Digest,* December 1995.

Truth in Poetry, Michael J. Bugeja, Poetry column in *Writer's Digest,* June 1996.

— *An Invitation* —

With the purchase of **Release the Poet Within!** (and *after* you have edited one of your poems according to the checklists in Chapter 7) you may tear out this sheet and mail it with one of your poems (and an SASE) to Leona Choy for a *free critique* of your poem.

Bonus! You are eligible to receive a *SPECIAL DISCOUNT* on Leona's three poetry books all under one cover titled *Celebrate the Moment!*

[ ] A poem and SASE are enclosed for Leona Choy's *FREE* critique.

[ ] I would like to order copies of Leona's poetry book *Celebrate the Moment!* at my special discount. Regular price: $14.95, discount price $12.00.

Leona's chapbook of computer poems, *Divine Applications*, FREE with my order.

Please add $2.00 for postage and handling.
(Virginia residents add 4.5% sales tax)

My name _____

Address _____

City _____ State _____ Zip _____

Total amount enclosed: $ _____

Make check or money order payable to Leona Choy.
Mail to: *Golden Morning Publishing,*
P.O. Box 2697 Winchester, VA 22604
Phone 540-877-1813   E-mail: leona@wtrm.org

— *An Invitation* —

With the purchase of **Release the Poet Within!** (and *after* you have edited one of your poems according to the checklists in Chapter 7) you may tear out this sheet and mail it with one of your poems (and an SASE) to Leona Choy for a *free critique* of your poem.

Bonus! You are eligible to receive a *SPECIAL DISCOUNT* on Leona's three poetry books all under one cover titled *Celebrate the Moment!*

[ ] A poem and SASE are enclosed for Leona Choy's *FREE* critique.

[ ] I would like to order copies of Leona's poetry book *Celebrate the Moment!* at my special discount. Regular price: $14.95, discount price $12.00.

Leona's chapbook of computer poems, *Divine Applications*, FREE with my order.

Please add $2.00 for postage and handling.
(Virginia residents add 4.5% sales tax)

My name _____

Address _____

City _____ State _____ Zip _____

Total amount enclosed: $ _____

Make check or money order payable to Leona Choy.
Mail to: *Golden Morning Publishing*,
P.O. Box 2697 Winchester, VA 22604
Phone 540-877-1813   E-mail: leona@wtrm.org

Order Information

Release the Poet Within!
How to Launch and Improve Poetry Craft and Ministry
by Leona Choy

$14.95 plus $2.00 shipping
(Virginia residents add 4.5% sales tax to all orders)

You may request orders drop-shipped to your friends. Write for discount information on quantity copies for your groups.

Available on Audio Cassette!
Leona's unabridged reading of
Release the Poet Within!
(2 cassette album)
$16.95 plus $2.00 shipping

Order from: Golden Morning Publishing
P.O. Box 2697, Winchester, VA 22604
Phone (540) 877-1813 or
E-mail: leona@wtrm.org
View Leona's Homepage with the latest book titles at:
http://www.wtrm.org/leona